Populism: A Very Short Introduction

VERY SHORT INTRODUCTIONS are for anyone wanting a stimulating and accessible way into a new subject. They are written by experts, and have been translated into more than 45 different languages.

The series began in 1995, and now covers a wide variety of topics in every discipline. The VSI library now contains over 510 volumes—a Very Short Introduction to everything from Indian philosophy to psychology and American history and relativity—and continues to grow in every subject area.

Very Short Introductions available now:

Available soon:

GRAVITY Timothy Clifton
VOLTAIRE Nicholas Cronk
MILITARY STRATEGY
   Antulio J. Echevarria II

INTELLECTUAL PROPERTY
   Siva Vaidhyanathan
ANIMAL BEHAVIOUR
   Tristram D. Wyatt

For more information visit our web site

www.oup.com/vsi/

Cas Mudde and Cristóbal Rovira Kaltwasser

POPULISM

A Very Short Introduction

OXFORD
UNIVERSITY PRESS

OXFORD
UNIVERSITY PRESS

Oxford University Press is a department of the University of Oxford.
It furthers the University's objective of excellence in research, scholarship,
and education by publishing worldwide. Oxford is a registered trade mark of
Oxford University Press in the UK and certain other countries.

Published in the United States of America by Oxford University Press
198 Madison Avenue, New York, NY 10016, United States of America.

Library of Congress Cataloging-in-Publication
Names: Mudde, Cas, author. | Rovira Kaltwasser, Cristóbal, author.
Title: Populism : a very short introduction / Cas Mudde and
Cristóbal Rovira Kaltwasser.
Description: Oxford ; New York, NY : Oxford University Press, 2017. |
Series: Very short introductions | Includes bibliographical
references and index.
Identifiers: LCCN 2016033957| ISBN 9780190234874 (paperback :
acid-free paper) | ISBN 9780190234881 (ebook updf) |
ISBN 9780190234898 (ebook epub) |
ISBN 9780190234904 (online resource)
Subjects: LCSH: Populism. | Democracy. |
BISAC: POLITICAL SCIENCE / General.
Classification: LCC JC423 .M743 2017 | DDC 320.56/62—dc23
LC record available at https://lccn.loc.gov/2016033957

7 9 8

Printed in Great Britain
by Ashford Colour Press Ltd., Gosport, Hants.
on acid-free paper

To Maryann and Sofia

Contents

List of illustrations

Acknowledgments

We are grateful to the many colleagues and friends who have read (parts of) the manuscript and who have given us relevant feedback. They include Ben Stanley, Carlos de la Torre, Jan-Werner Müller, Kenneth Roberts, Kirk Hawkins, Luke March, Maryann Gallagher, Matthijs Rooduijn, Paul Lucardie, Petr Kopecký, Sarah de Lange, and Tjitske Akkerman. We also presented parts of the manuscript at the University of Amsterdam (March 2015) and the Aristotle University of Thessaloniki (June 2015), and we have benefited from the constructive criticism of the participants at both events. We further profited from the two sets of anonymous reviewers, who provided feedback on the book proposal and the full manuscript, as well as from the support of the team at Oxford University Press, most notably Nancy Toff and Elda Granata. Edgard Berendsen and Cristóbal Sandoval have also been of great help throughout the production process.

Cas wishes to acknowledge support from the Kellogg Institute for International Studies at the University of Notre Dame, where he was able to learn about populism outside of the European context during a one-year fellowship in 2009–2010. He is also grateful to the School of Public and International Affairs of the University of Georgia for granting him leave to undertake research in spring 2015, which enabled him to work on the book and discuss and present first drafts with colleagues around the world. Finally, he expresses his deepest thanks to Jan Jagers, a former PhD student and current friend who has provided crucial input in developing his understanding of populism.

Cristóbal wishes to acknowledge support from the Chilean National Fund for Scientific and Technological Development (FONDECYT project 1140101) and the Chilean Millennium Science Initiative (project NS130008). He also acknowledges support from Diego Portales University and the German Academic Exchange Service (DAAD), which allowed him to undertake a stay during July and August 2015 at the Social Science Research Center Berlin (WZB) to work on this manuscript. Finally, he also wishes to thank Rossana Castiglioni and Manuel Vicuña in Santiago de Chile as well as Wolfgang Merkel and Gudrun Mouna in Berlin, who have supported this project.

Chapter 1
What is populism?

Populism is one of the main political buzzwords of the 21st century. The term is used to describe left-wing presidents in Latin America, right-wing challenger parties in Europe, and both left-wing and right-wing presidential candidates in the United States. But while the term has great appeal to many journalists and readers alike, its broad usage also creates confusion and frustration. This book aims to clarify the phenomenon of populism and to highlight its importance in contemporary politics.

It offers a specific interpretation of populism, which is broadly shared but far from hegemonic. Its main strength lies in offering a clear definition of populism that is able to both capture the essence of most of the political figures who are generally described as populist and yet distinguish between populist actors from nonpopulist actors. Hence, it counters two of the main criticisms of the term, namely (1) that it is essentially a political *Kampfbegriff* (battle term) to denounce political opponents; and (2) that it is too vague and therefore applies to every political figure.

We position populism first and foremost within the context of liberal democracy. This choice is more informed by empirics and theory than by ideology. Theoretically, populism is most fundamentally juxtaposed to liberal democracy rather than to

1

democracy per se or to any other model of democracy. Empirically, most relevant populist actors mobilize within a liberal democratic framework, i.e., a system that either *is* or *aspires to be* liberal democratic. Although this focus is particular, and obviously limiting, it means that we neither consider liberal democracy to be flawless, or any alternative democratic system by definition undemocratic, nor apply the approach only within a liberal democratic framework.

An essentially contested concept

While no important concept is beyond debate, the discussion about populism concerns not just what it is, but whether it even exists. It truly is an essentially contested concept. A perfect example of the conceptual confusion is found in the seminal volume *Populism: Its Meaning and National Characteristics* in which different contributors define populism, among others, as an ideology, a movement, and a syndrome. To make things even more complicated, in different world regions populism tends to be equated, and sometimes conflated, with quite distinct phenomena. For instance, in the European context populism often refers to anti-immigration and xenophobia, whereas in Latin America it frequently alludes to clientelism and economic mismanagement.

Part of the confusion stems from the fact that populism is a label seldom claimed by people or organizations themselves. Instead, it is ascribed to others, most often with a negative connotation. Even the few rather consensual examples of populism, like the Argentine president Juan Domingo Perón or the murdered Dutch politician Pim Fortuyn, did not self-identify as populists. As populism cannot claim a defining text or a proto-typical case, academics and journalists use the term to denote very diverse phenomena.

While our so-called ideational approach is broadly used in a variety of academic disciplines, as well as more implicitly in much journalism, it is but one of several approaches to populism. An exhaustive overview of all the different approaches goes well beyond the possibilities, and purpose, of this short book, but we do want to mention the most important alternatives, which are more commonly used in certain academic disciplines or geographical regions.

The popular agency approach holds populism to mean a democratic way of life built through popular engagement in politics. It is particularly common among historians in the United States and among authors of volumes on the original North American populists—adherents of the Populist Party—of the late 19th century. Perhaps best represented in Lawrence Goodwyn's *Democratic Promise: The Populist Moment in America*, the popular agency approach considers populism essentially as a positive force for the mobilization of the (common) people and for the development of a communitarian model of democracy. It has both a broader and a narrower interpretation of populist actors than most other approaches, including almost all progressive mass movements.

The Laclauan approach to populism is particularly current within political philosophy, so-called critical studies, and in studies of West European and Latin American politics. It is based on the pioneering work of the late Argentinian political theorist Ernesto Laclau, as well as on his more recent collaborative work with his Belgian wife Chantal Mouffe, in which populism is considered not only as the essence of politics, but also as an emancipatory force. In this approach liberal democracy is the problem and radical democracy is the solution. Populism can help achieve radical democracy by reintroducing conflict into politics and fostering the mobilization of excluded sectors of society with the aim of changing the status quo.

The socioeconomic approach was particularly dominant in studies of Latin American populism during the 1980s and 1990s. Economists such as Rudiger Dornbusch and Jeffrey Sachs have understood populism primarily as a type of irresponsible

What is populism?

economic policy, characterized by a first period of massive spending financed by foreign debt and followed by a second period marked by hyperinflation and the implementation of harsh economic adjustments. While the socioeconomic approach has lost support in most other social sciences, largely because later Latin American populists supported neoliberal economics, it remains current among economists and journalists, particularly in the United States. In a more popular form "populist economics" refers to a political program that is considered irresponsible because it involves (too) much redistribution of wealth and government spending.

A more recent approach considers populism, first and foremost, as a political strategy employed by a specific type of leader who seeks to govern based on direct and unmediated support from their followers. It is particularly popular among students of Latin American and non-Western societies. The approach emphasizes that populism implies the emergence of a strong and charismatic figure, who concentrates power and maintains a direct connection with the masses. Seen from this perspective, populism cannot persist over time, as the leader sooner or later will die and a conflict-ridden process for his replacement is inevitable.

A final approach considers populism predominantly as a folkloric style of politics, which leaders and parties employ to mobilize the masses. This approach is particularly popular within (political) communication studies as well as in the media. In this understanding, populism alludes to amateurish and unprofessional political behavior that aims to maximize media attention and popular support. By disrespecting the dress code and language manners, populist actors are able to present themselves not only as different and novel, but also as courageous leaders who stand with "the people" in opposition to "the elite."

Each individual approach has important merits, and various aspects are compatible with our own ideational approach. Hence, we do not disregard these approaches here out of disagreement; rather, we seek to provide one clear and consistent approach throughout this short book. We believe this will help the reader better understand this highly complex but important phenomenon, even if through a specific lens.

An ideational approach

The long-standing debate over the essence of populism has led some scholars to argue that populism cannot be a meaningful concept in the social sciences, while others consider it primarily as a normative term, which should be confined to media and politics. While the frustration is understandable, the term *populism* is too central to debates about politics from Europe to the Americas to simply do away with. Moreover, it is feasible to create a definition that is able to accurately capture the core of all major past and present manifestations of populism, while still precise enough to exclude clearly nonpopulist phenomena.

In the past decade a growing group of social scientists have defined populism predominantly on the basis of an "ideational approach," conceiving it as a discourse, an ideology, or a worldview. While we are far from securing a consensus, ideational definitions of populism have been successfully used in studies across the globe, most notably in western Europe, but increasingly also in eastern Europe and the Americas. Most scholars who adhere to the ideational approach share the core concepts of our definition, if not necessarily the peripheral concepts or the exact language.

Beyond the lack of scholarly agreement on the defining attributes of populism, agreement is general that all forms of populism include some kind of appeal to "the people" and a denunciation of "the elite." Accordingly, it is not overly contentious to state that populism always involves a critique of the establishment and an adulation of the common people. More concretely, we define populism as *a thin-centered ideology that considers society to be ultimately separated into two homogeneous and antagonistic camps, "the pure people" versus "the corrupt elite," and which argues that politics should be an expression of the* volonté générale *(general will) of the people.*

Defining populism as a "thin-centered ideology" is helpful for understanding the oft-alleged malleability of the concept in question. An ideology is a body of normative ideas about the nature of man and society as well as the organization and purposes of society. Simply stated, it is a view of how the world is and should be. Unlike "thick-centered" or "full" ideologies (e.g., fascism, liberalism, socialism), thin-centered ideologies such as populism have a restricted morphology, which necessarily appears attached to—and sometimes is even assimilated into—other ideologies. In fact, populism almost always appears attached to other ideological elements, which are crucial for the promotion of political projects that are appealing to a broader public. Consequently, by itself populism can offer neither complex nor comprehensive answers to the political questions that modern societies generate.

This means that populism can take very different shapes, which are contingent on the ways in which the core concepts of populism appear to be related to other concepts, forming interpretative frames that might be more or less appealing to different societies. Seen in this light, populism must be understood as a kind of mental map through which individuals analyze and comprehend political reality. It is not so much a coherent ideological tradition as a set of ideas that, in the real world, appears in combination with quite different, and sometimes contradictory, ideologies.

The very thinness of the populist ideology is one of the reasons why some scholars have suggested that populism should be conceived of as a transitory phenomenon: it either fails or, if successful, "transcends" itself into something bigger. The main fluidity lies in the fact that populism inevitably employs concepts from other ideologies, which are not only more complex and stable, but also enable the formation of "subtypes" of populism. In other words, although populism as such can be relevant in specific moments, a number of concepts closely aligned to the morphology of the populist ideology are in the long run at least as important for the endurance of populist actors. Hence, populism seldom exists in pure form. Rather, it appears in combination with, and manages to survive thanks to, other concepts.

One of the main critiques against ideational definitions of populism is that they are too broad and that they can potentially apply to all political actors, movements, and parties. We agree that concepts are useful only if they not only include what is to be defined, but also *exclude* everything else. In other words, our definition of populism only makes sense if there is non-populism. And there are at least two direct opposites of populism: elitism and pluralism.

Elitism shares populism's basic monist and Manichean distinction of society, between a homogeneous "good" and a homogeneous "evil," but it holds an opposite view on the virtues of the groups. Simply stated, elitists believe that "the people" are dangerous, dishonest, and vulgar, and that "the elite" are superior not only in moral, but also in cultural and intellectual terms. Hence, elitists want politics to be exclusively or predominantly an elite affair, in which the people do not have a say; they either reject democracy altogether (e.g., Francisco Franco or Augusto Pinochet) or support a limited model of democracy (e.g., José Ortega y Gasset or Joseph Schumpeter).

Pluralism is the direct opposite of the dualist perspective of both populism and elitism, instead holding that society is divided into a broad variety of partly overlapping social groups with different ideas and interests. Within pluralism diversity is seen as a strength rather than a weakness. Pluralists believe that a society

7

should have many centers of power and that politics, through compromise and consensus, should reflect the interests and values of as many different groups as possible. Thus, the main idea is that power is supposed to be distributed throughout society in order to avoid specific groups—be they men; ethnic communities; economic, intellectual, military or political cadres, etc.—acquiring the capacity to impose their will upon the others.

Likewise, it is important to establish the fundamental difference between populism and clientelism, as these terms are often conflated in the literature (particularly with regard to Latin American politics). Clientelism is best understood as a particular mode of *exchange* between electoral constituencies and politicians, in which voters obtain goods (e.g., direct payments or privileged access to employment, goods, and services) conditioned on their support for a patron or party. Without a doubt, many Latin American populist leaders have employed clientelist linkages to win elections and remain in power. However, they are not the only ones to do this, and there is no reason to think that populism has a particular affinity to clientelism. While the former is first and foremost an ideology, which can be shared by different political actors and constituencies, the latter is essentially a strategy, used by leaders and parties (of different ideologies) to win and exercise political power.

The only probable similarity between clientelism and populism is that both are unrelated to the left-right distinction. Neither the employment of clientelistic party-voter linkages nor the adherence to left or right politics is something that defines populism. Depending on the socioeconomic and sociopolitical context in which populism emerges, it can take different organizational forms and support diverse political projects. This means that the thin-centered nature of populism allows it to be malleable enough to adopt distinctive shapes at different times and places. By way of illustration, Latin American populism appeared mostly in a neoliberal guise in the 1990s (e.g., Alberto Fujimori in Peru), yet in a mainly radical left variant in the 2000s (e.g., Hugo Chávez in Venezuela).

Core concepts

Populism has three core concepts: the people, the elite, and the general will.

The people

Much of the debate around the concept and phenomenon of populism centers on the vagueness of the term "the people." Virtually everyone agrees that "the people" is a construction, at best referring to a specific interpretation (and simplification) of reality. Consequently, various scholars have maintained that this vagueness renders the concept useless, while others have looked for more specific alternatives, such as "the heartland." However, Laclau has forcefully argued that it is exactly the fact that "the people" is an "empty signifier" that makes populism such a powerful political ideology and phenomenon. Given that populism has the capacity to frame "the people" in a way that appeals to different constituencies and articulate their demands, it can generate a shared identity between different groups and facilitate their support for a common cause.

While "the people" is a construction, which allows for much flexibility, it is most often used in a combination of the following three meanings: the people as sovereign, as the common people, and as the nation. In all cases the main distinction between "the people" and "the elite" is related to a secondary feature: political power, socioeconomic status, and nationality, respectively. Given that virtually all manifestations of populism include some combination of these secondary features, it is rare to find cases in which only one of the mentioned meanings of the people comes to the fore.

The notion of the people as sovereign is based on the modern democratic idea that defines "the people" not only as the ultimate source of political power, but also as "the rulers." This notion is closely linked to the American and French Revolutions, which, in the famous words of U.S. president Abraham Lincoln, established "a government of the people, by the people, and for the people." However, the formation of a democratic regime does not imply that the gap between governed and governors disappears completely. Under certain circumstances, the sovereign people can feel that they are not being (well) represented by the elites in power, and, accordingly, they will criticize—or even rebel against—the political establishment. This could set the stage for a populist struggle "to give government back to the people."

In other words, the notion of 'the people as sovereign' is a common topic within different populist traditions, which functions as a reminder of the fact that the ultimate source of political power in a democracy derives from a collective body, which, if not taken into account, may lead to mobilization and revolt. Indeed, this was one of the driving forces behind the U.S. People's Party (also called the Populist Party) at the end of the 19th century, as well as other populist manifestations in the United States during the 20th century and today.

A second meaning is the idea of "the common people," referring explicitly or implicitly to a broader class concept that combines socioeconomic status with specific cultural traditions and popular values. Speaking of "the common people" often refers to a critique of the dominant culture, which views the judgments, tastes, and values of ordinary citizens with suspicion. In contrast to this elitist view, the notion of "the common people" vindicates the dignity and knowledge of groups who objectively or subjectively are being excluded from power due to their sociocultural and socioeconomic status. This is the reason why populist leaders and constituencies often adopt cultural elements that are considered markers of inferiority by the dominant culture. For example, Perón promulgated new conceptions and representations of the political community in Argentina that glorified the role of previously marginalized groups, in general, and of the so-called shirtless ones (*descamisados*) and blackheads (*cabecitas negras*), in particular.

To address the interests and ideas of "the common people" is indeed one of the most frequent appeals that we can detect in different experiences that are usually labeled as populist. It is worth noting that this meaning of the people tends to be both integrative and divisive: not only does it attempt to unite an angry and silent majority, but it also tries to mobilize this majority against a defined enemy (e.g., "the establishment"). This anti-elitist impetus goes together with a critique of institutions such as political parties, big organizations, and bureaucracies, which are accused of distorting the "truthful" links between populist leaders and "the common people."

The third and last meaning is the notion of the people as the nation. In this case, the term "the people" is used to refer to the national community, defined either in civic or in ethnic terms—for example, when we speak about "the people of Brazil" or "the Dutch people." This implies that all those "native" to a particular country are included, and that together they form a community with a common life. Accordingly, various communities of "people" represent specific and unique nations that are normally reinforced by foundational myths. Nevertheless, the definition of the boundaries of the nation is anything but simple. To equate "the people" with the population of an existing state has proven to be a complicated task, particularly because different ethnic groups exist on the same territory.

The elite

Unlike "the people," few authors have theorized about the meanings of "the elite" in populism. Obviously, the crucial aspect is morality, as the distinction is between the *pure* people and the *corrupt* elite. But this does not say much about *who* the elite are. Most populists not only detest the political establishment, but they also critique the economic elite, the cultural elite, and the media elite. All of these are portrayed as one homogeneous corrupt group that works against the "general will" of the people. While the distinction is essentially moral, the elite are identified on the basis of a broad variety of criteria.

First and foremost, the elite are defined on the basis of power, i.e., they include most people who hold leading positions within politics, the economy, the media, and the arts. However, this obviously excludes the populists themselves, as well as those within these sectors that are sympathetic to the populists. For example, the Austrian Freedom Party (FPÖ) would regularly critique "the media" for defending "the elite" and not treating the FPÖ fairly, but with one notable exception: *Die Kronen Zeitung*. This popular tabloid, read by almost one in five Austrians, was for a long time one of the staunchest supporters of the party and its late leader, Jörg Haider, and it was therefore considered a true voice of the people.

Because of the fundamental anti-establishment position of populism, many scholars have argued that populists can, by definition, not sustain themselves in power. After all, this would make them (part of) "the elite." But this ignores both the essence of the distinction between the people and the elite, which is moral and not situational, and the resourcefulness of populist leaders. From former Slovak premier Vladimír Mečiar to late Venezuelan president Hugo Chávez populists in power have been able to sustain their anti-establishment rhetoric by partly redefining the elite. Essential to their argument is that the *real* power does not lie with the democratically elected leaders, i.e., the populists, but with some shadowy forces that continue to hold on to illegitimate powers to undermine the voice of the people. It is here that "the paranoid style of politics," as the famous progressive American historian Richard Hofstadter described populism, most clearly comes to the fore.

Not unrelated to the definitions of the people, described above, the elite would be defined in economic (class) and national (authentic) terms. While populists defend a post-class world, often arguing that class divisions are artificially created to undermine "the people" and keep "the elite" in power, at times they do define the elite in economic terms. This is mostly the case with left-wing populists, who try to merge populism with some vague form of socialism. However, even right-wing populists relate the ultimate struggle between the people and the elite to economic power, arguing that the political elite are in cahoots with the economic elite, and putting "special interests" above the "general interests" of the people. This critique is not necessarily anti-capitalist either; for example, many Tea Party activists in the United States are staunch defenders of the free market, but they believe that big business, through its political cronies in Congress, corrupts the free market through protective legislation, killing competition and stifling small businesses, considered the true engines of capitalism and part of "the people."

Linking the elite to economic power is particularly useful for populists in power, as it allows them to "explain" their lack of political success; i.e., they are sabotaged by the elite, who might have lost political power but who continue to hold economic power. This argumentation was often heard in post-communist eastern Europe, particularly during the transitional 1990s, and it is still popular among contemporary left-wing populist presidents in Latin America. For instance, president Chávez often blamed the economic elite for frustrating his efforts at "democratizing" Venezuela, while Greek prime minister Alexis Tsipras, leader of the left populist Coalition for the Radical Left (Syriza), accused "the lobbyists and oligarchs in Greece" of undermining his government (incidentally, neither allegation was unfounded).

Populists also often argue that the elite is not just ignoring the interests of the people; rather, they are even working against the interests of the country. Within the European Union (EU) many populist parties accuse the political elite of putting the interests of the EU over those of the country. Similarly, Latin American populists have for decades charged that the political elites defend the interests of the United States rather than those of their own countries. And, combining populism and anti-Semitism, some populists believe the national political elites are part of the age-old anti-Semitic conspiracy, accusing them of being "agents of Zionism." For example, in eastern and central Europe leading politicians of right-wing populist parties such as Attack in Bulgaria and the Movement for a Better Hungary (Jobbik) have accused the national elites of being agents of Israeli or Jewish interests.

Finally, populism can be merged completely with nationalism, when the distinction between the people and the elite is both moral and ethnic. Here the elite are not just seen as *agents* of an alien power, they are considered alien themselves. Oddly enough, this rhetoric is not so much prevalent among the xenophobic populists in Europe, given that the elite (in whatever sector) is almost exclusively "native." Leaving aside the anti-Semitic rhetoric in eastern Europe, ethnic populism (or "ethnopopulism") is most evident in contemporary Latin America. For example, Bolivian president Evo Morales has made a distinction between the pure "mestizo" people and the corrupt "European" elites, playing directly at the racialized power balance in Bolivia.

While the key distinction in populism is moral, populist actors use a variety of secondary criteria to distinguish between the people and the elite. This provides them flexibility that is particularly important when populists acquire political power. Though it would make sense that the definition of the elite would be based upon the same criteria as that of the people, this is not always the case. For example, xenophobic populists in Europe often define the people in ethnic terms, excluding "aliens" (i.e., immigrants and minorities), but they do not argue that the elite are part of another ethnic group. They do argue, however, that the elite favors *the interests* of the immigrants over those of the native people.

1. Sarah Palin became prominent after her nomination as the 2008 Republican vice presidential candidate in the United States. Although she has been influential in the populist Tea Party movement, the group has maintained a not always smooth relationship with the Republican Party.

In many cases populists will combine different interpretations of the elite and the people, i.e., class, ethnicity, and morality. For example, contemporary American right-wing populists such as Sarah Palin and the Tea Party describe the elite as latte-drinking and Volvo-driving East Coast liberals; contrasting this, implicitly, to the real/common/native people who drink regular coffee, drive American-made cars, and live in Middle America (the heartland). Pauline Hanson, leader of the right-wing populist One Nation party, would juxtapose the true people of rural Australia, proud of their British settler heritage, to the intellectual urban elite, who "want to turn this country upside down by giving Australia back to the Aborigines."

General will

The third and last core concept of the populist ideology is the notion of the general will. By making use of this notion, populist actors and constituencies allude to a particular conception of the political, which is closely linked to the work of the famous philosopher Jean-Jacques Rousseau (1712–1778). Rousseau distinguished between the general will (*volonté générale*) and the will of all (*volonté de tous*). While the former refers to the capacity of the people to join together into a community and legislate to enforce their common interest, the latter denotes the simple sum of particular interests at a specific moment in time. Populism's monist and moral distinction between the pure people and the corrupt elite reinforces the idea that a general will exists.

Seen in this light, the task of politicians is quite straightforward: they should be, in the words of the British political theorist Margaret Canovan, "enlightened enough to see what the general will is, and charismatic enough to form individual citizens into a cohesive community that can be counted on to will it." Chávez provided a prime example of this populist understanding of the general will in his 2007 inaugural address:

Nothing . . . is in greater agreement with the popular doctrine then to consult with the nation as a whole regarding the chief points upon which governments, basic laws, and the supreme rule are founded. All individuals are subject to error and seduction, but not the people, which possesses to an eminent degree of consciousness of its own good and the measure of its independence. Because of this its judgment is pure, its will is strong, and none can corrupt or even threaten it.

By employing the notion of the general will, many populists share the Rousseauian critique of representative government. The latter is seen as an aristocratic form of power, in which citizens are treated as passive entities, mobilized periodically by elections, in which they do nothing more than select their representatives. In contrast, they appeal to Rousseau's republican utopia of self-government, i.e., the very idea that citizens are able to both make the laws and execute them. Not surprisingly, beyond the differences across time and space, populist actors usually support the implementation of direct democratic mechanisms, such as referenda and plebiscites. By way of illustration, from Peru's former president Alberto Fujimori to Ecuador's current president Rafael Correa, contemporary populism in Latin America is prone to enact constitutional reforms via constituent assemblies followed by referendums.

Hence, it can be argued that an elective affinity exists between populism and direct democracy, as well as other institutional mechanisms that are helpful to cultivate a direct relationship between the populist leader and his/her constituencies. To put it another way, one of the practical *consequences* of populism is the strategic promotion of institutions that enable the construction of the presumed general will. In fact, adherents of populism criticize the establishment for their incapacity and/or disinterest in taking into account the will of the people. And this critique is often not without reason. For instance, populist parties of the left and the right in Europe condemn the elitist nature of the project of the European Union (EU), while contemporary left populists in Latin America criticize the (former) elite for ignoring the "real" problems of the people.

Rather than a rational process constructed via the public sphere, the populist notion of the general will is based on the notion of "common sense." This means that it is framed in a particular way, which is useful for both aggregating different demands and identifying a common enemy. By appealing to the general will of the people, populism enacts a specific logic of articulation, which enables the formation of a popular subject with a strong identity ("the people"), which is able to challenge the status quo ("the elite"). From this angle, populism can be seen as a democratizing force, since it defends the principle of popular sovereignty with the aim of empowering groups that do not feel represented by the political establishment.

However, populism also has a dark side. Whatever its manifestation, the monist core of populism, and especially its notion of a "general will," may well lead to the support of authoritarian tendencies. In fact, populist actors and constituencies often share a conception of the political that is quite close to the one developed by the German political theorist Carl Schmitt (1888–1985). According to Schmitt, the existence of a homogeneous people is essential for the foundation of a democratic order. In this sense, the general will is based on the unity of the people and on a clear demarcation of those who do not belong to the demos and, consequently, are not treated as equals. In short, because populism implies that the general will is not only transparent but also absolute, it can legitimize authoritarianism and illiberal attacks on anyone who (allegedly) threatens the homogeneity of the people.

Some commentators go so far as to argue that populism is essentially anti-political because populist actors and constituencies seek to create anti-political utopias, in which, supposedly, no dissent exists between (or within) "we, the people." This is perfectly captured in Paul Taggart's notion of "the heartland"—the populist's imagined community and territory that portrays a homogenous identity that allegedly is authentic and incorruptible. But this is only part of the picture. Claiming to oppose "political correctness" and break the "taboos" imposed on the people by the elite, populists promote the repoliticization of certain topics, which either intentionally or unintentionally are not (adequately) addressed by the establishment, such as immigration in western Europe or the policies of the so-called Washington Consensus in Latin America.

The advantages of the ideational approach

Adopting an ideational approach, we have defined populism as a thin-centered ideology, which has come to the fore not only in different historical moments and parts of the world, but also in very different shapes or "subtypes." While populism has been conceptualized in other ways, such as a multiclass movement or a specific type of mobilization or political strategy, the ideational approach has several advantages over alternative approaches, which will be developed in more detail in the following chapters.

First, by conceiving of populism as a thin-centered ideology, it is possible to understand why populism is so malleable in the real world. Due to its restricted ideological core and concepts, populism necessarily appears attached to other concepts or ideological families, which are normally at least as relevant to the populist actors as populism itself. Most notably, political actors have combined populism with a variety of other thin- and thick-centered ideologies, including agrarianism, nationalism, neoliberalism, and socialism.

Second, contrary to definitions that limit populism to a specific type of mobilization and leadership, the ideational approach is able to accommodate the broad range of political actors normally associated with the phenomenon. Populist actors have mobilized in many different manners, including through loosely organized social movements as well as through tightly structured political parties. Similarly, while a certain type of leadership is prevalent, populist leaders come in many different shapes and sizes. They all do have one thing in common, however: a carefully crafted image of the vox populi.

Third, the ideational approach is uniquely positioned to provide a more comprehensive and multifaceted answer to the crucial question in debates on populism: what is its relationship with democracy? The relationship between populism and democracy is not as straightforward as its many opponents or its few protagonists claim. The relationship is complex, as populism is both a friend *and* a foe of (liberal) democracy, depending on the stage of the process of democratization.

Fourth, and finally, defining populism as an ideology allows us to take into account both the demand side and the supply side of populist politics. Where most accounts focus exclusively on the populist supply, as they define populism as a style or strategy used by the political elite, our approach enables us to also look at the populist demand, i.e., the support for populist ideas at the mass level. This helps us to develop a more comprehensive understanding of both the causes of populist episodes and the costs and benefits of democratic responses to populism.

Chapter 2
Populism around the world

Scholars of populism share the idea that it is a modern phenomenon. Conventional wisdom holds that populism emerged in the late 19th century in Russia and the United States and is closely related to the spread of democracy as both an idea and a regime. Today populism affects almost all continents and political regimes, even if it is most prevalent in the democracies of Europe and the Americas. While all populists share a common discourse, populism is an extremely heterogeneous political phenomenon. Individual populist actors can be left or right, conservative or progressive, religious or secular.

Some observers see this extreme diversity as a reason to reject the term populism altogether, arguing that anything so diverse lacks substance. But rather than reflecting a lack of core attributes, the diversity of populist actors is a consequence of the fact that populism rarely exists in isolation. Given that populism is a thin-centered ideology, addressing only a limited set of issues, almost all populist actors combine populism with one or more other ideologies, so-called host ideologies. Broadly speaking, most left-wing populists combine populism with some form of socialism, while right-wing populists tend to combine it with some type of nationalism.

Each populist actor emerges because of a particular set of social grievances, which influences its choice of host ideology, which in turn affects how the actor defines "the people" and "the elite." As national political contexts are often strongly shaped by regional or even global developments, populist actors in specific regions or periods can be very similar. For example, in the current European context the overarching political context of the European Union (EU) shapes much of the national politics, including populist politics—virtually all populist actors within the EU are Euroskeptic, even if the specific character and intensity of the skepticism differs.

In this chapter we provide a concise overview of the main populist actors of the past 150 years. We focus, in particular, on the three geographical areas in which populism has been most relevant: North America, Latin America, and Europe. We shortly describe the political context, the characteristics and host ideology, and the specific interpretation of the people and the elite of the populists in these regions in key moments. We end by noting several recent populist actors outside these traditional areas, most notably in Asia, the Middle East, and sub-Saharan Africa.

North America

North America, and particularly the United States, has a long history of populist mobilization, going back to the late 19th century. Although the continent has had its share of populist leaders, often at the state level—such as Governor Huey Long in Louisiana or Premier Preston Manning in Alberta—almost all significant populist forces have been characterized by movements with relatively weak central leadership and organization. From the agrarian revolt of the late 19th century to the Occupy Wall Street and Tea Party movements of the early 21st century, populism in North America has often emerged spontaneously and been characterized by regional mobilization and weak organization.

At the end of the 19th century the frontier states of North America went through important economic and social transitions.

Infrastructural developments, such as the extension of the railway system, and economic changes, such as the coining of silver, affected the rural areas particularly hard. A mix of agrarianism and populism gave way to the so-called prairie populism of the late 19th and early 20th centuries. While strongest in the western provinces of Canada and in the Southwest and Great Plains regions in the United States, populist sentiments were widespread throughout North America during this period.

The prairie populists of that time understood "the people" to be farmers, more specifically yeomen, free and independent farmers of European descent. In line with producerism, which has always informed populism in North America, farmers were depicted as the pure people, those who tilted the land and produced all the goods of society (notably clothing and food). The elite were the bankers and politicians in the Northeast, who produced nothing yet extorted goods from the farmers through high credits on loans. While the original populists manifested some anti-Semitic and racist streaks, the distinction between the people and the elite was not primarily of an ethnic or religious nature. Rather, the basis was moral, geographical, and occupational, i.e., between the good, rural farmers and the corrupt, urban bankers and politicians.

Within the federal systems of Canada and the United States populist parties and politicians were able to gain significant local and regional influence and success, but they lacked a national political presence. The People's Party, publicly known as the Populists, had representatives in the legislatures of several states in the 1890s. Still, lacking a single leader with cross-regional appeal, the People's Party decided to support the official candidate of the Democratic Party, William Jennings Bryan, for the presidential election of 1896. Populism lost most of its momentum after Bryan lost the election, but it would reappear periodically within the broader Progressive movement in the early 20th century. In Canada several regional Social Credit parties gained significant electoral successes and political offices from Alberta to Quebec from the 1930s until the 1960s, but the federal Social Credit Party of Canada (the Socreds) was plagued by regional divisions and never grew into a dominant national force.

Populism returned with a vengeance in the anti-communist movement of the early Cold War period. Influenced by the insecurities of the times, and by the longstanding fear and rejection of left-wing ideas within American conservatism, an amorphous right-wing mass movement transformed U.S. populism from a primarily progressive into a predominantly reactionary phenomenon. For the anti-communist populists "the people" were the common and patriotic ("real") Americans from the heartland, whereas "the elite" lived in the coastal areas, notably the Northeast, and covertly or overtly supported "un-American" socialist ideas. Linking populism to producerism, in which the pure people are squeezed between a corrupt elite above them and a racialized underclass below them, they accused the elite of mooching off the hard work of the people and of "redistributing" their wealth to the non-white underclass to stay in power.

The anti-communist movement largely disappeared from public view in the 1970s, as the excesses of the anti-communist witch-hunts of McCarthyism—named after Senator Joseph McCarthy (R-WI)—became broadly known and the rise of a policy of détente and increasing U.S. superiority vis-à-vis the Soviet Union weakened the paranoid fear of a communist takeover. Populism's broad popular appeal was not lost on some mainstream Republican politicians, however, who tried to tap into the right-wing rage among average Americans. One of the most skillful was Richard Nixon, the later disgraced 37th president of the United States. While not a populist at heart, Nixon popularized the term "silent majority" as a reference to the majority of the (real) American people figuratively and literally silenced by the (liberal) elite.

Right-wing populism was also at the heart of the two most successful third-party presidential campaigns of the late 20th century. In 1968 former Democratic governor George C. Wallace of Alabama ran as the candidate of the American Independent Party (AIP), winning almost 10 million votes, or 13.5 percent of those cast. Running essentially a single-issue campaign in defense of segregation, in which his producerist populism targeted both the African American poor below and the anti-segregationist white elites above, Wallace carried five states in the South. In 1992 Texas billionaire Ross Perot would do even better, winning almost 20 million votes, 18.9 percent of the ballots cast. His "United We Stand, America" campaign combined a broad range of right-wing concerns and issues, such as the budget deficit and gun control, with moderate producerism and strong populism. Using folksy language to pit the pure heartland against the corrupt East Coast, Perot promised the (real) American people that he would "clean out the barn" in Washington. His 1996 campaign, as leader of the newly founded Reform Party, was much less successful; still, he attracted 8 million voters, 8.4 percent of the ballots cast.

While the main "enemy within" of right-wing populists has changed somewhat through time—for instance, the communists in the 1950s were replaced by the civil rights movement in the 1960s and the "activist judges" in the 1970s—the main socioeconomic and, even more important, sociocultural grievances have remained remarkably constant: "our way of life" is attacked by the "liberal elite" who use an oppressive (federal) state and a far too expensive and expansive welfare state to stifle the initiative and values of the people while providing "special privileges" to non-deserving minorities. This discourse has informed all major right-wing populist campaigns in North America, from the more racist AIP of Wallace of the 1960s to the more neoliberal Reform Parties of Perot and Manning of the 1990s.

Although populism has moved from more progressive in the 19th century to more conservative in the 20th century, the self-definition of "the people" has changed little. They are still mostly the common people from the heartland, with perhaps a more inclusive interpretation in terms of occupation (middle class rather than peasantry) and religion (Christian rather than Protestant). In contrast, the depiction of "the elite" has changed somewhat. While big business and politicians from the Northeast are still central to the populist discourse, an alleged cultural elite has become more prominent. In essence, this cultural "liberal elite" works through (higher) education, particularly the Ivy League universities, where they "pervert" the bureaucrats, judges, and politicians of the future with "un-American" ideas.

The first decade of the 21st century has seen the emergence of two new populist movements, both propelled into action by social grievances related to the Great Recession. While they span the political spectrum, the two movements have a lot in common. They strongly oppose the government bailouts of the bank sector, initiated under Republican president George W. Bush and continued under his Democratic successor Barack Obama. In long-standing U.S. fashion they claim to defend a pure "Main Street" against a corrupt "Wall Street." However, they are divided by their host ideology, which makes Occupy Wall Street more inclusionary and the Tea Party more exclusionary in terms of both the people and the elite.

Claiming to speak for "the 99%" who lost out as a consequence of the economic crisis, i.e., "the" American people, the Occupy movement emerged as a left-wing protest to the Bush/Obama bailout and the close ties between Wall Street and Washington, the corrupt 1 percent elite. While Occupy Wall Street attracted most media attention, physically occupying Zuccotti Park in the Manhattan Financial District, similar groups occupied locations throughout North America (and beyond). Occupy merged a progressive social justice agenda with populism, which led to an inclusive interpretation of "the people" and only weak producerism. It considered the economic and political elite as one homogeneous block, of which the mainstream media elite also constituted a part. While aspects of its rhetoric have survived, such as the populist division of the 99 percent versus the 1 percent in the rhetoric of Democratic senator and presidential candidate Bernie Sanders, the Occupy movement itself has faltered as a consequence of a lack of central leadership, forceful removals, and the cold winter of 2011.

The Tea Party movement mainly mobilized conservatives and libertarians against the bailouts. It has a very strong producerist message, which leads to an often implicit, racialized interpretation of the people. While the Tea Party shares with the Occupy movement an aversion to Wall Street, its definition of "the elite" is more selective. Many Tea Party groups and supporters reserve the term for bankers, Democrats, and Hollywood. However, the movement has been weakened by fundamental tensions between the so-called Astroturf and grassroots sections. The former includes well-financed and organized lobby groups like FreedomWorks, which are close to the Republican establishment, while the latter entails the thousands of small local and regional Patriot and Tea Party groups throughout the country, which consider the Republican establishment to be RINOs (Republicans In Name Only). Both groups claim to express the voice of "we the people," but the populist sentiments of the grassroots groups are much more pronounced than those of the Astroturf, which mainly targets President Obama and the Democratic Party. Also, while the grassroots express mostly sociocultural grievances ("taking our country back"), the Astroturf focuses almost exclusively on socioeconomic grievances (such as "Obamacare" and tax hikes).

Latin America

Latin America is the region with the most enduring and prevalent populist tradition. The combination of high levels of socioeconomic inequality and relatively long periods of democratic rule explain to a great extent why populism is such a triumphant ideology in many Latin American countries. On the one hand, the concentration of economic and political power in a small minority makes the populist discourse particularly appealing, since it helps to identify the existence of a fraudulent oligarchy (*oligarquía*) that acts against the wishes of the people (*el pueblo*). On the other hand, the periodic realization of relatively free and fair elections provides a mechanism whereby voters can channel their dissatisfaction with the state of affairs. Consequently, we shouldn't be surprised that many Latin American citizens support populist parties and leaders who promise to establish a government in which the people rule themselves instead of being ruled by an oligarchy.

Although populism's electoral success across Latin America is related to the combination of democratic politics and extreme inequality, it is important to bear in mind that the region has seen the rise and fall of different versions of populism. Throughout the history of Latin America we can identify three waves of populism. Each of these different waves not only advanced a particular understanding of who is part of "the pure people" and "the corrupt elite," but also adopted specific ideological features that facilitated the construction of a narrative around the perceived social grievances.

The first wave of Latin American populism started with the onset of the Great Depression in 1929 and lasted until the rise of the so-called bureaucratic authoritarian regimes at the end of the 1960s. During this period of time, Latin American countries experienced a crisis of incorporation: the increasing migration of rural people to urban areas and the implementation of economic reforms leading to industrialization paved the way for the rise of demands for political and social rights. Throughout the region, different leaders and parties advanced political programs concerned with social issues. Socialism and communism gained ground in most Latin American countries, but in some of them populism turned out to be much more successful. This was the case in countries such as Argentina, Brazil, and Ecuador, where Getúlio Vargas, Juan Domingo Perón, and José María Velasco Ibarra, respectively, became presidents by developing a political language centered on "the people" rather than on the "working class." At the same time, they relied on the ideology of *Americanismo*, which claims that all Latin American inhabitants have a common identity and denounces the interference of imperial powers.

One important commonality of the different national expressions of the first wave of populism lies in the way in which "the pure people" and "the corrupt elite" were framed. All these populist experiments had clear corporatist tendencies, according to which the pure people was defined as a virtuous mestizo community composed of peasants and workers, neglecting the citizens of indigenous and African descent. Thanks to this image of the pure people, populist leaders were able to foster the mobilization and integration of excluded sectors as long as they expressed loyalty to the leader in question. With regard to the corrupt elite, all first wave populists spoke about a national oligarchy in alliance with imperialist forces that was against the economic import substitution industrialization model. In practice, this meant that not the whole establishment was depicted as the corrupt elite, but rather those elite sectors that were at odds with the governance model promoted by populist leaders.

The second wave of populism was much shorter and less prolific than the first. It emerged in the early 1990s and the most paradigmatic cases could be found in Argentina (Carlos Menem), Brazil (Fernando Collor de Mello), and Peru (Alberto Fujimori). Because these countries were suffering profound economic crises at the end of the 1980s, populist leaders were able to win elections by blaming the elite for the dramatic situation of the country and by proclaiming that the people had been robbed of their rightful sovereignty. Most of these leaders did not develop clear programmatic stances on how to confront the economic situation,

2. Eva Perón and her husband General Juan Domingo Perón were a glamorous power couple in Argentina in the 1940s and 1950s. He served as president of Argentina three times from the 1940s to the 1970s. By employing populist ideas, they gave voice to excluded sectors of Argentine society and are still venerated by many in Argentina today.

and, once in power, they opted to cooperate with the International Monetary Fund (IMF) to implement harsh neoliberal reforms. Although these measures were not popular, they helped to stabilize the economy and eliminate hyperinflation. This explains in part why populist leaders such as Menem and Fujimori were reelected.

By adopting a neoliberal set of ideas, the second wave of populism articulated a particular understanding of who belongs to "the pure people" versus "the corrupt elite." In contrast to the first wave, the struggle was framed as against the "political class" and the state. The alleged corrupt elite was depicted as those political actors who favored the existence of a strong state and opposed the development of a free market. The ideology of *Americanismo* and its emphasis on anti-imperialism did not play a role. In consonance with the neoliberal approach, the people were portrayed as a passive mass of individuals, whose ideas could be deduced from opinion polls. In practice, the second wave of populism was characterized by the implementation of anti-poverty programs targeted at the informal sectors and the extreme poor.

The third and current wave of Latin American populism was initiated by the electoral triumph of Hugo Chávez in Venezuela in 1998, one that subsequently spread to countries such as Bolivia (Evo Morales), Ecuador (Rafael Correa), and Nicaragua (Daniel Ortega). Because these leaders made use of *Americanismo* and anti-imperialist rhetoric, these cases have some similarity to the ones of the first wave. However, those active in the third wave of populism have shown a propensity to employ socialist ideas, to the point that the party founded by Evo Morales is called Movement toward Socialism (MAS) and the party established by Hugo Chávez is named the United Socialist Party of Venezuela (PSUV). This differs clearly from the first wave of populism, which tried to position itself beyond the left-right divide. All populist leaders in the third wave present themselves as radical leftists, who claim to fight the free market and who aim to construct a new development model that will bring real progress to the poor.

The appeal of this populist leftist discourse is related to the social grievances stemming from the neoliberal reforms that were implemented in Latin America during the last two decades of the 20th century. While generating macroeconomic stability, they did nothing to help reduce the high levels of socioeconomic inequality in almost all countries of the region. By politicizing the issue of inequality and condemning the elites in power, third wave populist actors have been able to become salient. Moreover, by combining socialist and populist ideas, these leaders have developed an inclusionary concept of the pure people: all those who are excluded and discriminated against. This is particularly evident in the case of Morales in Bolivia, who has advanced an "ethnopopulist" discourse that acknowledges the multiethnic character of the country but stresses the necessity of implementing policies in favor of the discriminated indigenous groups.

With regard to the corrupt elite, all third wave populists maintain that their countries have been governed by a fraudulent establishment that implemented the rules of the game in their own favor. As a consequence, they argue that the time has come to give sovereignty "back to the people" through the formation of a "constituent assembly" in charge of drawing up a new constitution, which has to be ratified via a referendum. All three leaders—Chávez, Correa, and Morales—have implemented this type of constitutional change as soon as they came to power. Recent developments have shown that the new constitutions not only diminished the power of the old elites, but also seriously constrained the capacity of the opposition to compete in a free and fair manner against the populist governments.

Europe

Populism has lived a relatively marginal existence in Europe in the 20th century, even though one of the two original agrarian populist movements emerged in Russia at the end of the 19th century. Russian populism (*narodnichestvo*) appeared in response to the hardship of the peasantry in feudal tsarist Russia. It called for democratic reforms to protect peasants from both landlordism and the commercialization of agriculture. But whereas U.S. populists were able to create a political mass movement, the Russian *narodniki* never grew beyond a small cultural movement of mainly urban intelligentsia. Between 1874 and 1877, the "Go to the People" movement dispersed to the countryside to mobilize "the people" against "the elite," but the peasantry largely rejected them. Their two main organizations, People's Will and Black Repartition, faltered after a young member of the first group assassinated Tsar Alexander II in 1881.

While the *narodniki* failed in Russia, they inspired many of the agrarian movements that existed in eastern Europe in the early 20th century. These movements shared an agrarian populism quite similar to the Populists in North America, in which the peasant was considered to be the main source of morality and agricultural life, the foundation of society. They vehemently opposed the urban elite and the centralizing tendencies and materialist basis of capitalism, arguing instead for the preservation of small family farms and for self-governance. The agrarian populists were popular in the rural areas of eastern Europe but remained largely excluded from political power in the authoritarian states that were run by an elite of landowners and the military.

Communism and fascism flirted with populism, particularly during their movement phases, in an attempt to generate mass support. In essence, however, both should be seen as ideologies and regimes that were elitist rather than populist. This is most evident in the case of fascism, which in its different varieties exalts the leader (*Führer*) and the race (National Socialism) or state (fascism) rather than the people. While communism has a more popular focus, Marxism-Leninism in particular has a strong elitist core, declaring the Communist Party the vanguard of the people (i.e., the working class), which leads rather than follows them. Moreover the fundamental ideas of "class struggle" and, particularly, "false conscienceless" are antithetical to populism.

Scholars agree that populism was almost totally absent from European politics during the first decades of the post–World

War II era. Eastern Europe was under the control of communist regimes, which exchanged a strong leader (Stalin) for a strong, if inefficient, bureaucracy, while western Europe was rebuilding its democracies on the basis of ideological moderation, frightened by both fascism and communism. Some isolated populist movements appeared, which mainly expressed a conservative rural backlash against centralization and politicization of the agricultural sector. Among the few successful populist parties was the Union for the Defense of Traders and Artisans (UDCA) of Pierre Poujade in France. While contesting only one national election successfully, in 1956, the so-called Poujadists have had a lasting effect on French politics. In fact, the term *poujadism* has become synonymous for populism well beyond France.

It was only in the late 1990s that populism became a relevant political force in Europe. Responding to frustrations over the effects of both older and newer transformations of European politics and society, such as European integration and immigration, populist radical right parties emerged across the continent, though with different levels of electoral and political success. These parties combine populism with two other ideologies: authoritarianism and nativism. Whereas the former refers to the belief in a strictly ordered society, and is expressed in an emphasis on "law and order" issues, the latter alludes to the notion that states should be inhabited exclusively by members of the native group ("the nation") and that non-native ("alien") elements are fundamentally threatening to the homogenous nation-state. Hence, the xenophobic nature of current European populism derives from a very specific conception of the nation, which relies on an ethnic and chauvinistic definition of the people. This means that populism, authoritarianism, and nativism are experiencing a kind of marriage of convenience in Europe nowadays.

The prototypical populist radical right party is the National Front (FN) in France, founded in 1972 by Jean-Marie Le Pen, a former

UDCA parliamentarian. Le Pen transformed the unorganized and elitist French far right into a well-organized populist radical right party, which inspired parties and politicians across Europe. Le Pen claimed to "say what you think" and pitted the FN against "the Gang of Four," i.e., the four established parties at that time. Populist radical right parties also combine nativism and populism in their economic agenda of welfare chauvinism and their foreign policy agenda of Euroskepticism. They accuse the elite of destroying the welfare state to incorporate the immigrants, their alleged new electorate, and call for a welfare state for their "own people" first. With regard to foreign policy, they attack their national elite for allegedly "selling out" their country and people to the EU, a "bureaucratic, socialist, undemocratic Moloch" that serves only a cosmopolitan elite.

In addition to the nativist populist radical right, which tends to emerge from nationalist subcultures, several neoliberal populist parties, such as Forza Italia (FI) and the United Kingdom Independence Party (UKIP), emerged from the political mainstream. Frustrated by high taxes and rising costs of the welfare state, and the complicity of the mainstream right-wing parties, they advocate neoliberal policies of lower taxes and free trade with strong populist critiques of the political system and elites. Like their brethren in North America, they subscribe to producerism, albeit a more moderate interpretation, accusing the elite (i.e., mainstream parties and trade unions) of frustrating the hard-working common people with unnecessary laws and high taxes while rewarding their undeserving and unproductive electorate of public-sector workers and immigrants.

The end of communism unleashed populist sentiments throughout central and eastern Europe. In the few countries in which civil society played an important role in the overthrow of the communist regimes, such as East Germany and Poland, populist slogans like "we are the people" were prominent in the

3. Nigel Farage poses for the media with a pint of beer in a British pub. As the main leader in favor of the UK-EU membership referendum (Brexit), he aims to present himself as a British "common man" who is in tune with the ideas and interests of "the people."

"revolution." Populist sentiments were particularly strong in the founding elections, i.e., the first free and fair elections in post-communist eastern Europe, in which broad umbrella parties represented "the people" against "the elite" of the Communist Party. For example, the official slogan of the Czech umbrella party Civic Forum (OF) was "Parties are for party members, Civic Forum is for everybody." Most umbrella parties fell apart soon after the founding elections, which opened up space for smaller populist parties of the left, right, and center. Many were so-called flash parties—here today, gone tomorrow—linked to a specific personality. A prime example of an early post-communist populist flash party was Party X of the shady Canadian-Polish businessman Stanislaw Tyminski, who surprised everyone by coming in second in the 1990 presidential elections, losing out to the legendary leader of the anti-communist trade union Solidarity, Lech Walesa, in the second round.

As post-communist societies wrestled through the changes of the double (i.e., economic and political) transition—and in some cases even a third national transition, as new states were formed—new populist actors tried to tap into the growing political dissatisfaction with a discourse of "the stolen revolution." They accused the new democratic elites of being either part of the old communist elite or in cahoots with them. Consequently, they called for a new "real" revolution to oust the corrupt post-communist elite and finally give power to the people. Not surprisingly, this discourse has been particularly popular in countries that underwent a transition by pact, i.e., where democracy was the result of a pact between representatives of the communist regime and the democratic opposition. For example, both Hungarian Civic Alliance-Fidesz in Hungary and Law and Justice (PiS) in Poland have long claimed that the real revolution still has to take place. In fact, when Fidesz won a supermajority in 2010, it changed the constitution, arguing that "what we wanted to do in 1989, we were never able to do."

As populism remains mostly right-wing within Europe, the Great Recession has given a new momentum to left-wing populism. In Greece the economic devastation convinced a plethora of radical left groups to come together in the new left-wing populist Coalition of the Radical Left (Syriza), while in Spain the protests of the Outraged (*Indignados*) gave way to the birth of a new party, We Can (Podemos). This left-wing populism is fairly similar to that of the Occupy movement in North America, although each actor has its own specific enemies and terminology—for Syriza the EU is an important part of the elite, while Podemos mainly opposes "*la casta*," its derogative term for the national political elite. European left-wing populist forces tend to be Euroskeptic too, but more for social(ist) rather than national(ist) reasons. For instance, they strongly oppose the austerity measures imposed by the so-called Troika—i.e., the European Commission, the European Central Bank (ECB), and the International Monetary Fund (IMF).

Beyond the three main regions

Populism is growing in developing democracies in other parts of the world, most notably in Southeast Asia, the Middle East, and sub-Saharan Africa. Within these mostly electoral democracies, populism can be found both among ruling and among opposition forces. Given the even larger economic, social, and political diversity of these regions, it is harder to distinguish clear trends, although certain shared characteristics of populist actors can be determined.

The region with the clearest populist tradition is Australasia, more specifically Australia and New Zealand. Both countries have seen the rise of right-wing populist parties in the 1990s, very similar to the parties of that period in western Europe. New Zealand First (NZF) and One Nation (ONP) emerged out of growing frustration with increased immigration and with neoliberal welfare state reforms. Both parties claim to speak for the "native" population, but ONP defends the interests of the descendent of the white settlers of Australia, and it is critical of the indigenous Aboriginals, while NZF presents itself primarily as the voice of the indigenous Maori people of New Zealand.

In Southeast Asia populism appeared in the wake of the Asian economic crisis of 1997, which brought an abrupt end to the spectacular rise of the so-called Asian Tigers. Particularly in the developing democracies of the region, populist actors gave voice to widespread dissatisfaction with the now discredited old leaders and policies. Blending nationalism and populism, the populists attacked neoliberal "globalization" and the national elites who had implemented these policies. Populist "outsiders" like Joseph Estrada in the Philippines and Roh Moo-hyun in South Korea even managed to get elected to the presidency, though their tenure was relatively short and unsuccessful. The most extreme example of a "flash populist" was probably Chen Shui-bian, the "president of the people" in Taiwan, whose "government of the people" collapsed after just five months. The most prominent populist of Southeast Asia is undoubtedly Thaksin Shinawatra, who was ousted as prime minister of Thailand after large public protests and a military coup, but whose sister Yingluck has been able to continue his project.

Populism is fairly rare in Africa, where many countries are either still authoritarian or at best highly flawed electoral democracies. In contrast to most other regions, populism is mostly associated with authoritarian strongmen like Ugandan president Yoweri Museveni and Zambian president Michael Sata, whose populism was part of an intra-elite struggle for power. Museveni introduced a "no-party system," based on plebiscitarian instruments like referendums, and strongly opposed liberal democratic institutions like independent courts. When the Supreme Court declared one such referendum null and void, he responded in perfect populist fashion: "The government will not allow any authority, including the courts, to usurp the powers of the people." Even in the exceptional case of South Africa, one of the few liberal democracies on the continent, populism has emerged mostly from within the establishment. Julius Malema was a populist voice of opposition within the dominant African National Congress (ANC) who served as president of its Youth Organization from 2008 to 2012. However, because of his fiery rhetoric, problematic behavior, and polemical policy proposals, he was expelled from the ANC in 2012 and has since created a new party called the Economic Freedom Fighters (EFF).

Finally, while populism has been associated with some previous regimes in the Middle East, most notably those of Gamal Abdel Nasser in Egypt (1956–1970) and Muammar al-Gaddafi in Libya (1969–2011), it has become a more integral part of politics in the region only in the 21st century. In the more established democracies like Israel and Turkey populism is a characteristic of ruling and opposition parties and politicians alike, including long-term leaders Benjamin Netanyahu in Israel and Recep

Tayyip Erdogan in Turkey. And although the various "revolutions" that constituted what is now broadly known as the Arab Spring were not populist per se, populist rhetoric was central to the mobilization of many of its participants. The one slogan most associated with the Arab Spring, shouted at demonstrations from Tunisia to Egypt to Yemen, was "The people want to bring down the regime!"

Populism across time and space

In roughly 150 years populism has spread from a small elitist group in tsarist Russia and a broad but unorganized group in parts of the United States to a diverse political phenomenon that covers the globe. Its rise is closely linked to the rise of democracy in the world. While populism and democracy were relatively rare phenomena at the end of the 19th century, they are both widespread today. This is not to suggest that the two are necessarily connected; populism can exist within authoritarian regimes and many democracies do not have relevant populist actors. But as an ideology that exalts the general will of the people, populism profits from the growing global hegemony of the democratic ideal as well as from both the possibilities of electoral democracy and the frustrations with liberal democracy.

All political phenomena are products of a more or less specific cultural, political, and social context, and populism is no exception. This is why populism comes in a broad variety of forms. Which specific form populism ends up adopting is related to the social grievances that are dominant in the context in which it operates. Populist actors are experts in detecting and politicizing social grievances that, intentionally or not, are not being addressed adequately by the dominant political forces. But because populism is a very basic set of ideas, it necessarily appears in combination with a host ideology, which is crucial to offering a broader interpretation of the political context in order to attract the interests of large groups. It is the *combination* of populism and its host ideology that creates the specific interpretation of "the people" and "the elite." While this interpretation is typically related to the national context, particular regional phenomena can create waves of fairly similar populist actors, such as the populist radical right parties in contemporary Europe or the current variant of radical left populists in Latin America.

Chapter 3
Populism and mobilization

The definition advanced in this book does not tell us much about the ways in which political actors can use populism to mobilize the masses. By highlighting the existence of different types of populist mobilization we can better understand why certain populist experiences are electorally more successful, and longer lasting, than others. Before continuing, it is worth noting that populism is generally associated with a strong (male) leader, whose charismatic personal appeal, rather than ideological program, is the basis of *his* support. While charismatic (male) leaders are important to populism, populist mobilization is not always linked to a charismatic leader. Our short survey of past and contemporary examples of populist forces across the world shows that populism is associated with different forms of mobilization.

By mobilization we mean the engagement of a wide range of individuals to raise awareness of a particular problem, leading them to act collectively to support their cause. Overall, three types of populist mobilization can be identified: personalist leadership, social movement, and political party. While many populist actors can be neatly categorized in just one of these three categories, some have aspects of two or three, either at one time or over time. As these three types show, populist mobilization can be top-down (personalist leadership), bottom-up (social movement), or both (political party). How populist actors mobilize is partly determined by the political system they operate in, while the durability of their success is strongly affected by the type of mobilization.

Personalist leadership

The quintessential form of populist mobilization is that of an individual who, largely independent of an existing party organization, campaigns and gathers support on the basis of *his* personal appeal. Think of Rafael Correa in Ecuador, Pim Fortuyn in the Netherlands, Alberto Fujimori in Peru, Beppe Grillo in Italy, Ross Perot in the United States, or Thaksin Shinawatra in Thailand. In all these cases most supporters felt a personal(ized) connection to the leader, who mobilized purely top-down. The leaders connect directly to the supporters, largely unmediated through a strong political or social organization. While top-down mobilization is not unique to populist leaders, they are definitely more prone to it.

Where does this empirical affinity between populism and personalist leadership stem from? The answer to this question lies partly in the nature of the populist set of ideas, which considers both "the pure people" and "the corrupt elite" as homogeneous groups. Hence, the populist leader can claim to be the personification of *the* people (as, admittedly, could any other member of "the people"). In some cases the populist leader is not just the core of the political movement but also of its political identity; just think about Chavismo in Venezuela, Fortuynism in the Netherlands, and Peronism in Argentina.

In most cases, however, populist leaders do build some type of political organization around them, often seen as a necessary evil to be able to successfully contest elections. Technically speaking, this organization is a political party, i.e., a political group that presents one or more candidates for public office in elections. But in many cases the organization is largely a façade, as there are few members, committees, or internal structures. This is why we prefer to label this type of pseudo-organization a personalist electoral vehicle, i.e., a more or less ad hoc and powerless political structure that has been built, and is fully controlled, by a strong leader with the specific purpose of contesting elections.

By developing a personalist electoral vehicle, without being tied to a strong political organization, the populist leader can portray himself as a clean actor, who is able to be the voice of the "man in the street" since there are no intermediaries between him and "the people." For instance, Correa won the 2006 Ecuadorean presidential election by rejecting the establishment and creating a new political party that did not present candidates for Congress. Correa argued that political parties are fraudulent organizations. He promised to draft a new constitution by convening a constituent assembly, which had the task of constructing an institutional framework that allegedly respected popular sovereignty. A similar pattern of personalist mobilization can be seen in the case of Geert Wilders in the Netherlands, who constructed a political party that in reality is just a personalist electoral vehicle. As the sole member of the Party for Freedom (PVV) Wilders decides who is allowed to represent the party in various legislatures and how they should act and vote.

Although personalist leadership can be found around the world, it is more prevalent in certain regions, such as Latin America. Throughout the three waves of Latin American populism the modal type of mobilization has been personalist leadership, from Perón in the first wave through Fujimori in the second wave to Correa in the third wave. This is also the case in most non-Western countries where populists have successfully mobilized, such as South Korea and Taiwan. What these countries have in common is that they are developing democracies with a presidential system and relatively weak institutionalized political parties.

Example: Alberto Fujimori in Peru

At the end of the 1980s Peru faced not only a serious economic crisis, but also the rise of the Maoist guerrilla movement Shining Path. Under these circumstances, a completely unknown figure, Alberto Fujimori, rose to power by developing a populist campaign criticizing the establishment for the dramatic crisis threatening the country and presenting himself as a "pure" person, who wanted to get rid of the corrupt elite. By exalting his Japanese background, Fujimori framed himself as an outsider without links to the white elite and thus as someone who, like the majority of "the people," had experienced racial discrimination. Not by coincidence, one of the slogans of his campaign was "A President Like You." This slogan constituted a subtle attack against his main opponent, the famous writer Mario Vargas Llosa, a well-known member of the Peruvian cultural and political establishment, who won the Nobel Prize in Literature in 2010.

Fujimori was elected president in 1990, but he did not have a political party behind him and thus had no way of controlling Congress. He created a personalist electoral vehicle called Change 90, which was formed with the help of two minor organizations with little in common: an association of small entrepreneurs and a network of Protestant Evangelicals. The personnel working for Change 90 were so unimportant and inexperienced that Fujimori did not include a single member of the party in his first cabinet. He opted to govern with independents, active or retired military officers, and some individuals from other parties.

To wage the 1995 national elections, Fujimori created a new party called New Majority, which obtained a majority in Congress, but almost all legislators (MPs) were political novices handpicked by Fujimori and his confidants. After poor results in the 1998 municipal elections he decided to form yet another new political party for the 2000 national elections, this time called the Independent Front Peru 2000. In a heavily tainted process,

Fujimori was able to win the presidency but he could not secure a majority in Congress. As a consequence, he started to systematically bribe opposition MPs to support his government, which would become his downfall. Under investigation for bribery, Fujimori faxed his resignation as president during a visit to Japan, where he would stay for several years to evade prison in Peru.

All in all, Fujimori competed in elections with political organizations that were extremely weak and completely under his own control. Consequently, when his daughter Keiko decided to enter politics several years later, she was compelled to build her new political party practically from scratch, even though it includes some leaders who supported and worked in the *Fujimorista* government. Through the new party, Popular Force, Keiko Fujimori has been able to construct a common identity uniting local elites and grassroots organizations sympathetic to her father's government.

Social movement

Demonstrations, marches, and rallies are regular political phenomena in contemporary societies. They are examples of political mobilization in which individuals come together to put pressure on powerful actors. When protests are not episodic occurrences, but endure over time, we are dealing with a social movement. Social movements are usually described as informal networks (or "networks of networks") characterized by a continuous engagement of individuals and political groups that have a clear adversary and seek to promote collective action in the pursuit of a common objective. Iconic examples of (new) social movements include the U.S. Civil Rights movement of the 1960s and the western European environmental movements of the 1970s.

Social movements are informal networks that bring together people with a shared identity and a common opponent who engage in noninstitutionalized collective action to pursue a goal. Their preference for noninstitutionalized collective action, over the more usual electoral behavior, is often caused by the lack of access to the decision-making process. Therefore, social movements are different from both political parties and interest groups, which normally have a formal organization and participate on a regular basis in the decision-making process.

When it comes to defining a common identity and a common enemy, social movements have to develop a *frame* through which they identify the most important social grievances affecting society. In the process of frame construction, social movements normally resort to different ideological frameworks. For instance, the labor movement often employed Marxist ideas to construct a frame, in which the business community was portrayed as the common enemy and the workers were depicted as the aggrieved population. Nothing keeps social movements from using populism to construct a frame. However, this does not occur very often. Most social movements seek to develop a common identity for a *specific* group of individuals, such as students, women, workers, etc. In contrast, populism speaks about "the people" as one homogeneous category; it is a set of ideas that assumes that a *broad group* of individuals—though not the whole society—should act to regain its sovereignty, which has been stolen by a "corrupt elite." Consequently, populism is not very helpful for the construction of frames targeted at specific constituencies (i.e., subgroups of "the people").

An interesting aspect about populist social movements is that they are examples of bottom-up mobilization. In fact, populist social movements normally lack centralized leadership or a dominant leader—which is not necessarily to say that they are leaderless. Certain figures can play a significant role from time to time, but the key strength of a populist social movement relies on its capacity to interpret a widespread feeling of anger with the establishment and to convincingly propose that the solution lies in the sovereign people. As a consequence, events such as major corruption scandals involving high-ranking individuals from across different groups of the establishment or serious violations of the principle of popular sovereignty are propitious for the emergence of populist social movements. In contrast, political contexts in which specific groups feel discriminated against (e.g., youth) or aim to reform a limited policy sector (e.g., ecology) are not very conducive to the rise of populist social movements.

Looking at the contemporary world, the Great Recession has facilitated the rise of a wide variety of populist social movements across the globe. Occupy Wall Street in the United States and the so-called *Indignados* in Spain are good examples of this. Whereas the former developed the slogan "we are the 99%," the motto of the latter was "real democracy now—we are not goods in the hands of politicians and bankers." Both social movements had a clear populist tone, portraying "the political caste" (*la casta*) and the business community as "the corrupt elite" while defining the homogeneous people ("the 99%") as the only source of political legitimacy. And while both movements tried to develop a definition of "the people" that was inclusive to most marginalized minorities—including ethnic, religious, and sexual—its moral exclusion of "the elite," in terms of interests and values, was as essential as with the more exclusionary populist movements on the political right.

Example: The Tea Party in the United States

Although the groundswells of the movement go back much longer, many popular accounts place the origins of the Tea Party movement in the on-air rant of CNBC host Rick Santelli on the floor of the Chicago Mercantile Exchange in February 2009. Protesting the bailout policies of Democratic president Barack Obama, even though they were initiated by his Republican predecessor President George W. Bush, Santelli turned to the traders on the floor and shouted "It's time for another Tea Party," referencing the Boston Tea Party of 1773, an anti-tax protest against the British government that served as the prelude to the American Revolution. While this media event undoubtedly boosted the nascent movement, the Tea Party is in many ways just the newest form of conservative populist outrage in the United States.

The Tea Party movement was built upon a plethora of loosely organized grassroots right-wing populist activists, such as blogger Keli Carender (known as "Liberty Bell"), and groups, such as Tea Party Patriots, as well as professionally organized national conservative groups, such as Americans for Prosperity and FreedomWorks. The coalition of so-called grassroots and Astroturf groups was problematic from the outset, as many grassroots supporters considered the Astroturf professionals as part of the corrupt elite. Moreover, as the Tea Party became more closely associated with the Republican Party (GOP), not in the least because of the Astroturf groups, the more populist parts of the movement turned away from common national campaigns and directed their attention more to local and regional battles, particularly in the American Midwest and South.

But even the grassroots part of the Tea Party movement entails a great diversity of causes and groups, including those that are more libertarian, social conservative, religious fundamentalist, and white supremacist. Various aspiring leaders have emerged, ranging from right-wing television personality Glenn Beck to Congresswoman Michelle Bachman, but all are linked to specific subgroups, consequently finding at least as much opposition as support within the amorphous movement. Even former Alaska governor Sarah Palin, who had become a national and international celebrity after John McCain selected her as his running mate in 2008, got caught up in the fight between individual Tea Party groups, receiving strong criticism for charging huge speaker fees at (for profit) Tea Party group meetings.

Like other grassroots populist movements before it, the Tea Party quickly lost its national momentum, in part because of its lack of

4. The Tea Party is a populist movement that became influential in the United States after the onset of the Great Recession in the late 2000s. Its grassroots organizations, which are not directly controlled by elected politicians, organize gatherings such as this one in Mishawaka, Indiana, in 2009.

national leadership and organization, even if certain groups remain influential at the subnational level. Nevertheless, some GOP leaders who have been close to the Tea Party have been able to compete in the 2016 presidential primaries (e.g., Ted Cruz, Rand Paul, and Marco Rubio), even if much of the base has supported the GOP outsider Donald Trump, and it is an open question how much impact the Tea Party will have on both the GOP leadership and the party base in the near future.

Political party

The American political scientist E. E. Schattschneider famously proclaimed that you cannot have democracy without political parties. This is only a slight exaggeration. Contemporary democracy is undoubtedly a form of government that hinges upon political parties. They play at least three key functions in the democratic system. First, political parties are organizations that seek to aggregate the interests of different sectors of society. Second, political parties elaborate policy programs that work as their pledges to the voting public, who can evaluate these programs to decide whom to vote for in elections. Third, political parties invest time and resources to train personnel, who are crucial for both running elections as well as implementing the proposed reforms through public offices.

These three key functions of political parties are closely related to the very process of political representation. Modern democracies are a particular type of political regime in which voters are free to elect officials, who represent them by deciding matters on their behalf. These representatives are normally individuals working in political parties, i.e., political organizations that present candidates for public office in elections. As political parties compete for votes, they have to detect the issues that are salient to the electorate and create a corresponding policy program. In this process of discovering issues and constructing a program, party activists, members, and leaders interact closely. Consequently, the party is more than just a leader. Both the institution and the ideology may be linked to a strong leader, but they are not fully dependent upon one. Hence, parties often are able to survive a specific leader.

Given that populism is usually employed to attack the establishment, pundits and academics are prone to argue that it is against political representation. After all, populist actors and constituencies normally claim that existing political parties are corrupt organizations. This does not mean, however, that populism is intrinsically at odds with political representation. What populists want is to have *their* representatives in power, i.e., representatives of "the people." Accordingly, populist political parties use populism to challenge the establishment and to give voice to groups that feel unrepresented. In effect, the rise of populist parties and their electoral strength is directly related to their capacity to politicize certain issues, which intentionally or unintentionally are not being adequately addressed by existing political parties. As soon as populist parties become relevant and are able to own an issue, they win a space in the political landscape, forcing others parties to react and take their concerns into account. While social movement can do this too, the added ability to win votes (and seats) often makes populist parties more effective.

Despite the ideological tensions between populism and parties, political parties are the paradigmatic type of populist mobilization in much of Europe. Today a majority of European countries have at least one successful populist party; a populist party is among the three largest parties in roughly one-third of the countries. While some populist parties live up to the stereotype of the flash party, many of these are better categorized as ad hoc electoral vehicles constructed by personalist leaders than as real political parties. This applies both to the prototypical example of the Poujadist party and to more recent cases like the People's Movement for Latvia (TKL). Unsurprisingly, many of these parties are officially named after their leader, like the Austrian Team Stronach or the Dutch List Pim Fortuyn (LPF), or they are commonly known for their leader; for instance, TKL was more broadly known as the Siegerist Party, after party leader Werner Joachim Siegerist.

Many of the more relevant western European right-wing populist parties are relatively well-established organizations that have been around for two or more decades. Most notably, the Austrian Freedom Party (FPÖ) and Swiss People's Party (SVP) were founded in 1956 and 1971, respectively, and while both parties changed ideologically, they have maintained organizational continuity. But even "new" right-wing populist parties like the FN and Norwegian Progress Party (FrP) date back to the 1970s, while the Belgian Flemish Interest (VB) and Italian Northern

League (LN) were founded in the early and late 1980s, respectively. All these parties have slowly but steadily built and institutionalized a solid party organization with often several auxiliary organizations, such as youth branches. Even in eastern Europe, where few parties pre-date the fall of communism in 1989 and most parties are volatile and weak, some populist parties are quite stable and well organized. Examples include the left-wing populist Direction-Social Democracy (Smer) in Slovakia and the right-wing populist Law and Justice (PiS) in Poland.

Example: National Front in France

The National Front (FN) was founded as a coalition of a broad variety of far right *groupuscules*, ranging from the neo-fascist New Order to ultra-orthodox Catholics of the Lefebre sect, held together exclusively by the overpowering leadership of Jean-Marie Le Pen. After a slow beginning, during which the party was not much more than the sum of its parts, counting a mere 14,000 members in the mid-1980s, the FN set out to develop its own organization under the competent management of Bruno Mégret. It was hurt badly by a split between the Le Pen and Mégret camps in 1999, in which the party lost most of its competent party organizers and about two-thirds of its cadres. Experiencing a rebirth under Marine Le Pen, the FN has almost quadrupled its membership, from a mere 22,000 to some 83,000, since she succeeded her father as party leader in 2011.

Despite the nominally democratic party statutes, the power structure of the FN is extremely centralized. The party leader is elected by the party congress and can and does face serious competitors, but is extremely powerful once elected. Marine Le Pen exerts disproportionate influence through an extensive myriad of organizations headed by people appointed by, and responsible to, her. In fact, when she took over, her father was named "president for life," an honorary function that could not protect him from being thrown out of the party later on, after an increasingly public feud between father and daughter. Although the party congress had to approve his expulsion, and he had legal recourse within the party, Jean-Marie Le Pen was only saved by a civil court case that ruled in his favor and forced the FN to reinstate him.

Today the FN organization spreads across the whole territory of France, including its overseas territories. It has a strong and very active youth organization, the National Front of the Youth (FNJ), boasting some 25,000 members. The FN even has an organization for "French abroad," organized in eleven geographically organized branches, claiming members in eighty countries around the world. To become better connected with blue-collar workers, its strongest electorate, the party has created several trade unions, particularly for sectors that are traditionally sympathetic to FN ideals (e.g., police officers and prison guards). As the modest wins in trade union elections have been invalidated by the fiercely anti-FN traditional trade unions, the FN has embarked upon an increasingly successful strategy of "entryism," in which its members "infiltrate" traditional unions and their leadership.

A dynamic model

While most examples of populist mobilization fit neatly into one of these three types, at least at a specific point (or period) in time, in many cases populist mobilization is a process that goes through different stages. Almost all populist mobilization starts without a strong organizational structure, perhaps except when a populist leader takes over an existing, well-organized political party and transforms it from a nonpopulist into a populist party. Interestingly, this is an increasingly common trajectory in Europe.

Many of the successful European populist parties, both on the left and on the right, started out as nonpopulist parties. For instance, in Germany the populist party The Left (Die Linke) is the successor to the ruling party of the German Democratic Republic, the Socialist Unity Party (SED), which was an elitist Marxist-Leninist organization. Two of the most successful populist radical right parties in western Europe, the FPÖ in Austria and the SVP in Switzerland, started out as nonpopulist parties, although with significant populist factions. After being elected party leader, Jörg Haider and Christopher Blocher, respectively, transformed the established nonpopulist party into a populist radical right party. In exceptional cases a long-serving leader can transform a nonpopulist party into a populist party, as is the case with Viktor Orbán and Fidesz in Hungary.

While these examples show that leaders can be very powerful within populist parties, this does not mean that these organizations were personalist electoral vehicles of their leader. Even after their power grab and party transformation, which led to significant electoral successes, Haider and Blocher endured significant opposition from within their own party—both from populists and from nonpopulists. Within the FPÖ the opposition was so fierce that Haider eventually chose to leave "his" party to found a new one, the Alliance for the Future of Austria (BZÖ). Interestingly, outside of his regional stronghold of Carinthia, most of the voters remained loyal to the old party (FPÖ) and did not follow the old leader to the new party (BZÖ).

In most cases, however, populist mobilization is unrelated to an existing political organization. The common model is a personalist leader who constructs an ad hoc electoral vehicle, i.e., top-down mobilization around a strong populist leader. In many cases this mobilization is either unsuccessful or it falls apart shortly after achieving electoral breakthrough. Populist leaders who are able to mobilize more or less successfully for a few elections tend to build a political party, however halfheartedly and reluctantly, to consolidate their power and increase their effectiveness.

Despite their predominance many populist parties actually survive the founder-leader, even if they often go through a period of electoral decline and weak leadership. Some even move from one strong leader to another, as was the case in both the FN (from Jean-Marie Le Pen to Marine Le Pen) and the FPÖ (from Haider to Heinz-Christian Strache). In other cases, the death of the founder-leader can help to unite different factions with the aim of constructing a political party that seeks to keep the populist set of ideas alive. Examples of this can be found in Latin America, where the death of Perón paved the way for the consolidation of the Argentine Justicialist Party, while the death of Chávez seems to have contributed to the strengthening of the United Socialist Party of Venezuela.

Social movements are a fairly rare type of populist mobilization, although it is the modal type in the United States, from the agrarian populist movement of the late 19th century to the populist movements on the right and the left of the early 21st century. Like other social movements, populist social movements tend to be episodic and local in the absence of a strong national leader or organization. The recent Occupy Wall Street movement is a perfect example of populism that never outlived its short-lived social movement phase. Few populist social movements are able to last for more than a few years. Those that survive tend to have connections to more organized groups, like the Tea Party, and to the broad and diverse networks of right-wing local and national groups, including the Republican Party.

Once a populist social movement finds a strong leader tensions emerge between leader and movement. The movement will quickly lose momentum particularly if the leader is able to build a political party and attract a significant part of the key activists and media attention. This happened recently in India, where the populist social movement India against Corruption (IAC), which emerged in the wake of an unprecedented wave of high-level corruption in 2011, largely disappeared when Arvind Kejriwal, one member of its five-man leadership called "Team Anna," founded the Common Man Party (AAP) and started to contest elections with various levels of success. Similarly, the Spanish Indignados, which emerged in protest of rising inequality and corruption in 2011, was eclipsed by Podemos, which followed a manifesto signed by thirty intellectuals and personalities and, despite ideological resistance, is strongly focused on the party founder and leader, the political science professor Pablo Iglesias Turrión.

Finally, a very exceptional case can be found in contemporary Bolivia, where all three types of populist mobilization are simultaneously at play. Evo Morales is a personalist populist leader, who is strongly connected to social movements that opposed neoliberal policies and fought for a better representation of ethnic groups in the 2000s. Morales was elected president of the country in 2006 and the political party behind him, Movement toward Socialism (MAS), has close relationships with these social movements. At the same time, MAS is a strong political organization, which, despite its loyalty to Morales, has different factions and an institutional structure across the whole country. Important tensions exist between the three types of

5. Evo Morales is widely respected as Bolivia's first president to come from the indigenous population. He leads a populist government that has implemented major leftist reforms since his rise to power in 2006. Not by chance, his slogan reads, "Building the new Bolivia."

populist mobilization in the country. For example, at certain times social movements have forced Evo Morales to change his position on specific reforms. And while he continues to be the undisputed leader of the party, debate is ongoing within the party about who should replace him in the near future.

Conclusion

Populists mobilize in a variety of different ways. We discussed the three main types of populist mobilization: personalist leadership, social movement, and political party. Two important questions remain unanswered, however. First: Why are some types of populist mobilization more prevalent in certain places than in others? Second: Do these different types of populist mobilization have an impact on the electoral success of populism?

Let's begin by offering a preliminary answer to the first question. Populist actors do not operate in a political vacuum. Various political contexts set conditions and provide incentives that are more or less favorable to the three different types of populist mobilization. Having said that, probably the most relevant factor is whether populism comes to the fore in a presidential or in a parliamentary system. More generally, presidential systems strengthen personalist leadership, while parliamentary systems incentivize the emergence of political parties. Consequently, populist leaders without an attachment to a political party can gain prominence and even win the executive power in presidential systems. In fact, this has occurred several times in Latin America (e.g., Perón, Fujimori, Correa). By contrast, in parliamentary systems the person who controls the executive is nominated by one or more political parties represented in the parliament. It is therefore not a coincidence that almost all populist forces in Europe are more or less well-organized political parties.

When it comes to analyzing the rise of populist social movements, the distinction between presidential and parliamentary systems does not seem to be crucial. Rather, like other social movements, they will mainly develop in democracies that have a restricted "political opportunity structure" (POS). Among the more restrictive POS institutions are a majoritarian electoral system, a related two-party system, and high (financial) barriers to influence politics through elections or lobbying. Seen in this light, the predominance of the social movement type of populist mobilization in the United States makes sense. Although populist sentiments are widespread within U.S. society, politics is dominated by just two broad parties—the Republicans and the Democrats—that have been highly successful in preventing the rise of viable third parties. Although mainstream politicians in the United States regularly use populist rhetoric, populist mobilization is only really feasible outside of the party structure, in social movements like the Tea Party, that are often closely related to one of the two parties.

This leaves us to address the second question: Do the types of populist mobilization have a different impact on the electoral success of populism? To answer this question properly, it is important to bear in mind that electoral success can be defined in two different ways: *electoral breakthrough*, which refers to winning enough votes to enter the political arena (e.g., parliament or presidency), and *electoral persistence*, which means the ability to develop into a stable force within the political system.

Without doubt, populists can achieve electoral breakthrough through personalist leadership. This is particularly true when the populist leader is a charismatic figure, who has adequate credentials to portray him- or herself as an outsider and has the ability to establish a direct link with the masses. However, these types of leaders are usually very bad at building institutions. By constructing a personalist electoral platform, rather than a well-organized political party with competent activists and personnel, they have serious problems at succeeding in terms of electoral persistence. For instance, Alberto Fujimori was able to win three presidential elections, but his party disappeared once he left the country in the year 2000—forcing his daughter to try to build a political party from the ashes of her father's personalist electoral vehicle.

Given that populist political parties employ a radical language, they normally have to confront the reactions of mainstream political parties as well of civil society organizations and the media. The stronger these responses, the more difficult it is for populist parties to develop a well-functioning organization that recruits competent personnel. As a consequence, populist parties often achieve electoral breakthrough, but they fail at establishing electoral persistence. Some populist parties are able to survive big electoral defeats at the national level because of particular local or regional strongholds, from which the party can try to launch a national revival. Many European populist radical right parties have such local strongholds, such as the VB in Antwerp and the SVP in Zurich. The most extreme example was the Austrian BZÖ, whose national representation in the federal parliament was solely based on the phenomenal support in Haider's home state of Carinthia.

Populist social movements have an ambivalent impact on the electoral success of populism. The rise of a populist social movement certainly gives more visibility to the populist set of ideas, but this does not automatically lead to the electoral breakthrough of populist actors. For instance, there are no signs that the Occupy Wall Street movement has contributed significantly to the election of left-wing populist politicians—although it might have bolstered the campaigns of more progressive Democrats like Bernie Sanders and Elizabeth Warren. However, this is different when a strong populist social movement is connected to, or mobilizes partly within, an established political party, as is the case with the Tea Party and the Republican Party in the United States. While the Tea Party has not been able to gain control of the national party, it has played a major role in some primaries and has been instrumental in increasing the populist representation within Republican delegations in state and federal legislatures.

The biggest chance at electoral persistence, however, occurs when a populist social movement is able to either build a new political party or transform an existing one. In fact, many of the most successful political parties have arisen from social movements, which provide organizational resources that are crucial to establish well-functioning political parties. Just think about the influence of the labor movement in the rise of socialist and social democratic parties in Europe and Latin America. A paradigmatic example of a populist social movement triggering both the electoral breakthrough and the persistence of a populist party is MAS, whose leader Morales has won the last three consecutive presidential and parliamentary elections in Bolivia.

Chapter 4
The populist leader

Leaders are central to most political phenomena and populism is certainly no exception. Many scholars argue that, above and beyond its diverse manifestations, a defining feature of populism is its reliance on strong leaders who are able to mobilize the masses and/or conduct their parties with the aim of enacting radical reforms. It is true that many manifestations of populism have given rise to flamboyant and strong political leaders. From Venezuelan president Hugo Chávez to Dutch politician Geert Wilders, populism is often guided by strong leaders, who, through their behavior and speech, present themselves as the vox populi (voice of the people). This has led the British political scientist Paul Taggart to state that populism "requires the most extraordinary individuals to lead the most ordinary of people."

As populism is first and foremost a set of ideas, which can be employed by very different actors, there is no such thing as *the* prototypical populist leader. The charismatic strongman, the stereotypical populist leader in academic and popular writing, does describe some of the better known populist leaders, but such an individual is mostly successful in specific societies. Depending on the political culture of the country in which the populist leader mobilizes, her or his "extraordinary" nature lies in very specific and different features. What all populist leaders do have in common, however, is that they present themselves as the voice of the people, which means as both political outsiders and authentic representatives of the common people. This image is carefully constructed by the populist leader, based on a plethora of personal characteristics, and does not always reflect reality.

The charismatic strongman

In both academic and popular debates the populist leader is implicitly or explicitly defined as a charismatic strong*man*. In Latin America the stereotypical populist leader is the *caudillo*, a generic term with roots in the Latin *caput* (head), which normally alludes to a strong leader, who exercises a power that is independent of any office and free of any constraint. Populist strongmen tend to rule on the basis of a "cult of the leader," which portrays him as a masculine and potentially violent figure.

The link between populism and strongmen goes back to president Juan Domingo Péron of Argentina, the original populist *caudillo*, who is, for many, still the personification of Latin American populism. An army colonel turned civil politician, Péron served in both authoritarian and democratic governments. A more recent example of a populist strongman is the late Venezuelan president Hugo Chávez, another military man turned into a successful civil politician. Non–Latin American strongmen tend to lack a military background, but they share the other features. Examples include former Italian prime minister Silvio Berlusconi, former Slovak prime minister Vladimír Mečiar, and former Thai prime minister Thaksin Shinawatra.

While there is a close association between populist leaders and strongmen, it is important not to conflate the two. In fact, only a minority of strongmen are populists and only a minority of populists is a strongman. The notion of the strongman is often related to authoritarian regimes. Leaders like Juan Manuel de Rosas in Argentina (1793–1877), Porfirio Díaz in Mexico (1830–1915), and Francisco Franco in Spain (1892–1975) are common examples of strongmen in the scholarly literature. All these leaders can be considered as absolute rulers and thus anything but democrats. But as populism maintains an ambivalent relationship with democracy, the authoritarian characteristic of the strongman is not inherent to populism.

Many political leaders present themselves as a strong leader, but populist strongmen take it a step further, crafting an image of a man of action, rather than words, who is not afraid to take difficult and quick decisions, even against "expert" advice. Drawing upon anti-intellectualism and a sense of urgency, often largely created by the populist themselves, he will argue that the situation ("crisis") requires "bold action" and "common sense solutions." In an example of life imitating art, Philippine actor-turned-politician Joseph "Erap" Estrada even built his political image upon his movie characters, which all were heroic defenders of the poor and oppressed.

This image of the strongman is frequently combined with an emphasis on the virility of the populist leader. For example, Estrada responded to a young woman's claim that she was his illegitimate daughter by saying that this might well be true, as "many women want babies with me." Few populists have so passionately cultivated the image of the virile man as Silvio Berlusconi. While opponents tried to turn his infamous *bunga bunga* (sex) parties into political scandals, *il Cavaliere* (The Knight) used the media attention to emphasize his virility, only strongly denying the accusation that he had paid for sex with call girls at the parties. "For those who love to conquer, the joy and the most beautiful satisfaction is in the conquest. If you have to pay, what joy is there?" he once said in an interview.

Populist leaders in general, and strongmen in particular, also use simple and even vulgar language, a so-called *Stammtisch* (beer table) discourse. They present themselves as "one of the boys," a man's man, talking sports and women rather than politics and

6. Silvio Berlusconi was a polemical populist leader who served as prime minister of Italy several times during the 1990s and 2000s. In 2007 he launched his new political party, Il Popolo della Libertà (The People of Freedom), which fused together two previous existing right-wing political organizations: Forza Italia and Alleanza Nazionale.

policies. They relate to "the common man" by playing on sexist stereotypes and by using coarse language. A perfect example is the former leader of the Italian right-wing populist Northern League (LN), Umberto Bossi, who would excite crowds by saying that "the League has a hard-on" while literally giving the finger to Rome (i.e., the elite).

Perhaps the most contentious feature of the populist strongman is charisma. According to the great German sociologist Max Weber (1864–1920), charismatic leadership refers to the authority of the extraordinary and personal *gift of grace* (charisma), the absolutely personal devotion and personal confidence in revelation, heroism, or other qualities of individual leadership. Weber believed that charismatic leadership would thrive particularly in times of crisis, when people seek refuge in the specific characteristics of certain individuals, often political outsiders, rather than in the most common sources of authority (i.e., custom and statute). Weber's theory of charismatic leadership has strongly influenced scholarship on populism, although this is not always explicitly acknowledged.

The popular understanding of charisma is a set of extraordinary personal qualities of the leader, which are considered universal. What these features are, however, is a topic of intense debate and confusion. Terms such as "popular" and "strong" are often used to capture charisma, and thereby explain popularity, which tends to be tautological. Popular leaders are described as "strong" because of their popularity, while unpopular leaders are portrayed as "weak" because of their lack of popularity.

In a Weberian understanding, charismatic leadership is about a specific *bond* between leader and followers, which is defined at least as much by the expectations and perceptions of the followers as by the individual characteristics of the leader. Hence, it makes little sense to look for certain universal features of charisma. Rather, charisma and its individual features are culturally determined; what is considered charismatic in, say, Sweden will differ from what is considered charismatic in, say, Peru.

This notwithstanding, some fairly straightforward cases of charismatic populist leaders, who established a direct link with their supporters, can be cited. The most evident cases are populist leaders who have been able to gain significant popular support without the backing of a strong organization or clear political philosophy, such as former Brazilian president Collor de Mello or the late Dutch politician Pim Fortuyn. When populists are leaders of well-organized political parties with a well-defined program, it is more difficult to establish whether support is based on loyalty to the party, support for the program, or a charismatic bond with the leader. Stressing the importance of individual leaders for the electoral success of populist parties, commentators have come up with terms such as the "Le Pen effect" or the "Haider phenomenon." In both cases, however, the charisma of the leader seems to have had only a temporary effect, i.e., bringing (new) supporters into the party electorate. Once in, they were socialized into more solid support by both the party organization and the party ideology. This fact, rather than the charisma of the leaders, also explains the somewhat surprising finding that many of these parties have exceptionally loyal supporters, who stick with their party even after a change in leadership.

Some scholars have argued that charismatic leadership can be institutionalized within political organizations, leading to "charismatic parties" rather than mere charismatic leaders. Given the existing diversity in organizational structures, it would go too far, however, to argue that populist parties are by definition charismatic parties. Others have focused on the internal rather than the external effects of charismatic leadership, arguing that certain populist leaders have "coterie charisma," which ties an inner core of activists to a specific leader. This enables the "charismatic" leader to overcome internal divisions within a broader movement. Examples of populist leaders with strong coterie charisma would be FN leader Jean-Marie Le Pen, who single-handedly kept an extremely heterogeneous coalition of far right groups together, or Vladimir Zhirinovsky, founder-leader of the seriously misnamed Liberal Democratic Party of Russia (LDPR).

The vox populi

Given that populist politics is essentially a struggle of "the pure people" against "the corrupt elite," and pretends to defend popular sovereignty at any cost, it is crucial for populist leaders to present themselves as the true voice of the people. Just as "the people" and "the elite" are constructions, although usually based on a warped interpretation of reality, the vox populi is a construction of the populist leader—ironically often unwittingly reinforced by the anti-populist rhetoric of the establishment. This construction consists of two distinct but interrelated processes: (1) separation from the elite and (2) connection to the people. Whereas the former process is related to the outsider-status of populist leaders, the latter process is linked to their claimed authenticity.

Populist leaders have to convince their followers that they do not belong to the (corrupt) elite but are part of the (pure) people. The populist strongman does this by emphasizing action and masculinity, playing into cultural stereotypes of the people, and by proposing "common sense" solutions at odds with the opinion of experts. But other populist leaders have to be more creative. We will here illustrate how three groups of more unlikely populist actors portray themselves as voices of the people by using their gender, profession, and ethnicity.

Women

Despite the fact that the stereotype of the strong*man* continues to dominate the public perception of populism, there are many examples of female populist leaders. Probably the first famous female populist was Eva Péron (1919–1952), the second wife of Juan Domingo Péron, who continues to inspire ordinary

7. Marine Le Pen, leader of the French National Front, speaks in front of a statue of Joan of Arc during the 2011 May Day celebration in Paris. The location was far from coincidental, as the French National Front is a populist radical right party that has won success by redefining French nationhood.

Argentinians and famous foreigners alike (like U.S. pop singer Madonna). Some contemporary female populists are also related to populist strongmen, such as Marine Le Pen in France and Yingluck Shinawatra in Thailand. But many female populist leaders are self-made women who have built their own political careers. Probably the best example is Pauline Hanson, who founded the One Nation Party (ONP) in Australia and who was the main reason for the party's, admittedly short-lived, success. Other examples are Pia Kjærsgaard, the former leader of the Danish People's Party (DF); Frauke Petry, the current leader of the Alternative for Germany (AfD); Siv Jensen, the current leader of the Norwegian Progress party (FrP); and Sarah Palin, the firebrand ex-governor of Alaska.

Just like populist strongmen, female populist leaders draw upon gendered notions of society to construct their image of the vox populi. Most notably, they use their sex to construct their outsider status. The mere fact that a populist leader is female, whereas the vast majority of the (political) elite is male, strengthens her image as a political outsider. For example, Palin emphasized her opposition to "the good-ol' boys" network in Alaskan and U.S. politics. On top of that, gendered notions of society help female populists to present themselves as reluctant politicians. When she entered politics, Hanson declared, "I come here not as a polished politician, but as a woman who has had her fair share of life's knocks."

To connect themselves to the pure people, many female populists emphasize features of the "good woman," as defined by their culture, often presenting themselves primarily as mothers or wives. This helps them to appear as "authentic" and generate a bond with constituencies feeling ignored by the establishment. Palin famously coined the term "hockey mom," adjusting the more common term of "soccer mom" to her specific Alaskan context, as well as "mama grizzly," feeding off gendered stereotypes of the fiercely protective mother. In a particularly instructive gendered blend of nationalism and populism, Hanson stated: "I care so passionately about this country, it's like I'm its mother, Australia is my home and the Australian people are my children."

Entrepreneurs

Another rather common but largely ignored populist leader is the economic entrepreneur. Some of the most famous populists were successful businessmen who belonged to the richest people in their country before becoming the voice of the common people. Forbes estimated the family fortune of the Shinawatras at $1.6 billion in 2015, making them the tenth richest family in Thailand, while it assessed the wealth of the Berlusconi family at a staggering $7.8 billion, the sixth richest family in Italy. The fortune of Ross Perot, the populist candidate who obtained almost 20 percent of the vote in the 1992 U.S. presidential elections, is valued at roughly $3.7 billion, making him the 155th richest person in the United States in 2015.

Because populism is based on a frontal attack against the establishment, the combination of "entrepreneur-populist" is not always easy to sell. But given that the populist distinction between the people and the elite is not fundamentally based on socioeconomic criteria—like class or wealth—but rather on morality, entrepreneur-populists are able to use their business acumen to construct their status as a *political* outsider. They present themselves as honest and self-made businessmen who have made their fortune *despite* the corrupt politicians, not because of them! Moreover, entrepreneur-populists claim to be reluctant politicians, who, unlike professional politicians, did not enter politics to profit from it financially. In the always colorful words of Berlusconi: "I don't need to go into office for the power. I have houses all over the world, stupendous boats ... beautiful airplanes, a beautiful wife, a beautiful family ... I am making a sacrifice."

For entrepreneur-populists, it would seem that, at first sight, connecting to the people is an impossible task. After all, their everyday lives could not be further removed from that of the "common man" they claim to represent. The average Italian doesn't live in a completely renovated 17th-century country mansion, Villa Gernetto (Silvio Berlusconi), while the average Joe in the United States doesn't have a museum named in their honor, the Perot Museum of Nature and Science in Dallas, Texas, thanks to a $50 million gift (Ross Perot). However, they often use their wealth to connect to "the people" and bestow an aura of authenticity, for example through sports. Most famously, Berlusconi bought AC Milan, one of the most popular soccer teams in Italy and the world, while Thaksin owned, albeit for a short time, Manchester City. In addition, populist entrepreneurs have been presidents of major soccer teams in their respective countries, including Moïse Katumbi in the Democratic Republic of Congo (TP Mazembe), Bernard Tapie in France (Olympique de Marseille), Gigi Becali in Romania (Steaua Bucharest), and the late Jesús Gil y Gil in Spain (Club Atlético de Madrid).

Ethnic leaders

The relationship between ethnicity and populism is much more complex than many accounts portray. Particularly in Europe the two are often conflated, a direct consequence of the predominance of populist radical right parties that combine authoritarianism, nativism, and populism. In Latin America the term *ethnopopulism* denotes a particular type of populism, most notably related to mobilization by indigenous peoples. While both types of populism use ethnicity to establish their authenticity, they do it in fundamentally different ways. For the European populist radical right ethnicity is not part of the populist distinction between the people and the elite, who are part of the same ethnic group, but rather of the nativist distinction between "natives" and "aliens," in which the latter are considered to be part of neither the people nor the elite. In the case of Latin American ethnopopulism, on the other hand, the nation is defined as a multicultural unit, within which the people and elite are divided by both morality *and* ethnicity.

Evo Morales and his party MAS constitute the prototypical case of ethnopopulism. Morales is the first indigenous president of Bolivia, a country with a majority of indigenous people who have been systematically discriminated against. He has often used his ethnicity as proof of both his separation from the elite (outsider status) and his connection to the common people (authenticity). For instance, he usually argues that he descends from those who have inhabited the Americas for forty thousand years, whereas most members of the elite are of more recent European origin. Moreover, Morales often claims authenticity on the basis of his ethnicity, since he is a member of the Aymara, one of the two largest indigenous groups in Bolivia. One of his most famous statements is: "We Indians are Latin America's moral reserve." But, unlike ethnic populists in Europe, Morales and MAS are not exclusionary. In fact, the party has reached out not only to the Aymara and the Quechua—the two largest indigenous groups of the country—but also to mestizos and whites. As Morales once declared, "the most important thing is the indigenous people are not vindictive by nature. We are not here to oppress anybody—but to join together and build Bolivia, with justice and equality."

But the populist leader does not even have to be part of the ethnic majority. As we have seen, Fujimori became one of the most popular politicians in Peru despite being part of the small Japanese minority in the country. Given that Peru is a strongly racialized society, where the elite are mainly of European descent, Fujimori's status as an ethnic minority helped him to connect to the common people. As a fellow non-European Peruvian, he was included in the category of the excluded people. Moreover, belonging to an ethnic minority contributed to crafting an image of a political outsider of humble origins, who had risen thanks to personal talent rather than connections with the establishment. This image was reinforced by his main competitor, Mario Vargas Llosa, a well-known novelist who was white and of European descent.

The insider-outsider

As part of their status of political outsider, who has nothing in common with the political establishment, populist leaders often claim to be political novices. This assertion helps to separate themselves from both the unpopular policies of previous governments and the perceived corruption and incompetence of politicians in general. It also fits the image of the reluctant politician, who is favorably compared to the professional politicians of the mainstream. In sharp contrast to the professional "political class," a popular term of populists, the populist claims to be driven to engage in politics not by personal ambition but by a higher calling, namely to bring politics (back) to the people. In reality, most populist leaders are very much part of the national elite. They often belong to the same sociodemographic strata as the political elite, i.e., highly educated, (upper) middle-class, middle-aged males of the majority ethnicity. And many of them have been politically active for years.

For example, Greek prime minister Alexis Tsipras started out as a member of the Communist Youth of Greece, while Collor de Mello had been elected on the ticket of many different parties before he became president of Brazil. Similarly, Wilders was an influential backbencher in charge of foreign policy in the conservative People's Party for Freedom and Democracy (VVD) before starting his one-man PVV. A few even held government positions before reinventing themselves as populist outsiders: Rafael Correa was finance minister in the government of Alfredo Palacio in Ecuador, Joseph Estrada served as vice president under President Fidel V. Ramos in the Philippines, and Roh Moo-hyun was minister of maritime affairs and fisheries in the administration of President Kim Dae-jung in South Korea.

Other populists have become politically active as a consequence of family connections, sometimes literally growing up within a populist party. This is the case with many, but certainly not all, prominent female populists: Isabel Péron was the widow of Juan Domingo Péron, Marine Le Pen and Keiko Fujimori are daughters of Jean-Marie Le Pen and Alberto Fujimori, respectively, while (short-term FPÖ chairwoman) Ursula Haubner and Yingluck Shinawatra are the sisters of Jörg Haider and Thaksin Shinawatra, respectively. All of them "inherited" their position as populist leader. To be clear, inherited leadership is neither specific to populists nor to women. Many female nonpopulist leaders in South Asia "inherited" their position from their father (e.g., Benazir Bhutto) or husband (e.g., Sonia Gandhi), but so have many male politicians in the West (such as Belgian premier Charles Michel and former U.S. president George W. Bush).

Overall, one can distinguish between three types of populists: outsiders, insider-outsiders, and insiders. True outsiders are very rare. They have no significant links to the elite, broadly defined (i.e., including cultural and economic elites), and build their career completely outside of the political mainstream. Among the few more prominent populist outsiders are Hugo Chávez and Alberto Fujimori. Chávez was a relatively low-ranked officer in the Venezuelan army who gained national notoriety only because of a failed coup d'état in 1992. Fujimori was an academic and university president who had no political network when he first ran for president. True outsiders are probably more successful in more personalized and fluid political systems, such as the presidential systems in Latin America, than in more institutionalized and established political systems, like the party-dominated parliamentary systems in western Europe.

In reality, almost all successful populists are insider-outsiders: men and women who have never been members of the political elite, i.e., the inner circle of the political regime, but have (strong) connections to them. FPÖ leader Jörg Haider was a protégé of Bruno Kreisky, Austria's long-serving social democratic chancellor (1970–1983), while long-term Republican senator John McCain catapulted Sarah Palin onto the national stage. Similarly, Berlusconi built his media empire through his special connection with Bettino Craxi, leader of the Italian Socialist Party (1976–1993) and premier of Italy (1983–1987). In post-communist eastern Europe most prominent populists of the 1990s had been closely connected to the communist regime—for example, Corneliu Vadim Tudor, the late leader of the populist radical right Greater Romania Party (PRM), was a "court poet" of communist dictator Nicolae Ceaușescu, while Vladimir Zhirinovski founded the first officially sanctioned "opposition" party in the Soviet Union. Ironically, often it is these connections to the (former) elite that separate the successful populists from the unsuccessful populists.

Finally, there is a small group of insider populists, i.e., populists who come from within the heart of the political elite. Some have held high-ranking positions in mainstream parties before starting a second career as a populist politician. The best example is undoubtedly Thaksin Shinawatra, who served twice as vice prime minister before launching his own populist party and becoming prime minister. In other cases populist leaders transform not only themselves, but also their populist party. In Switzerland, Christoph Blocher changed the conservative SVP into the most successful populist radical right party in western Europe, while, in Hungary, Viktor Orbán has pushed the initially libertarian Fidesz toward conservatism first and right-wing populism later.

The boundaries between insider and outsider status become blurred when populist leaders are able to win elections and stay in power for a long period of time. When this occurs, they necessarily become part of the political—and usually also the economic—establishment. There is no better example of this than the case of Chavismo in Venezuela. Fifteen years of governing the "Bolivarian revolution" has led to an almost wholesale elite change and the rise of a new ruling class, the so-called *Boliburguesía*. This even changed the status of Chávez, who, after more than ten years in power, transformed from a genuine outsider in the 1999 presidential elections to a true insider in the elections of 2013.

Just as the boundaries between insider and outsider are sometimes blurred, the distinction between populist and nonpopulist politician is not always easy to discern. Some famous mainstream politicians have used populist rhetoric from time to time, including Australian prime minister Tony Abbott and U.S. president Ronald Reagan. In fact, commentators tend to use the term *insider populism* in reference to this particular type of politician. However, neither these politicians nor their parties were truly populist, as populism was not a core feature of their ideology. These insiders merely *used* populist rhetoric to set themselves apart from other mainstream politicians and (try to) look authentic. Not by chance, mainstream politicians tend to employ populist discourse mostly during election campaigns, while largely ignoring it in government.

The populist image

Personalization is a general trend in contemporary politics and populism is certainly no exception to this rule. Most of the successful cases of populism involve a strong leader, irrespective of the type of mobilization. But populism is neither defined by nor wedded to a specific type of leader. The stereotypical populist strongman constitutes only a minority of all populist leaders—irrespective of the host ideology of the populist actor. Moreover, the success of populist leaders is less dependent upon a universal list of specific personality characteristics than on a carefully constructed image of vox populi, based on the combination of outsider-status and authenticity.

The attractiveness of the specific image of the voice of the people is linked to the political culture of the society in which the populist leader operates. For example, the stereotypical populist strongman is more likely to be attractive to people in societies with a more traditional and machismo culture, while entrepreneur-populists will probably be attractive in more capitalist and materialist societies. Political culture has a particularly interesting effect on female populist leaders. Obviously, all societies are gendered, but they are not always gendered in the same way. Female populists can succeed in both emancipated and traditional societies, but in different ways. Traditional cultures will favor inherited female (and male) populist leaders, while emancipated societies will (also) be open to self-made female leaders.

The construction of the image of vox populi is also dependent upon the host ideology of the populist leader. For example, it is much easier to combine an entrepreneurial image with neoliberal populism than with socialist populism, while ethnic minorities can more easily become leaders of ethnopopulist than of populist radical right movements. Similarly, female leaders will probably construct a more traditional image in right-wing populist parties than in left-wing populist ones. All this notwithstanding, most populist leaders devote so much attention to constructing an image of political outsider in order to hide a long and close relationship to the same elites they so vehemently renounce. Hence, building upon Paul Taggart's original observation, populism can be thought of as *politics for ordinary people by extraordinary leaders who construct ordinary profiles*.

Chapter 5
Populism and democracy

The relationship between populism and democracy has always been a topic of intense debate. Although we are far from reaching a consensus, it is not far-fetched to suggest that the conventional position is that populism constitutes an intrinsic danger to democracy. Probably the most famous recent proponent of this position is the French intellectual Pierre Rosanvallon, who argues that populism should be conceived of as "a perverse inversion of the ideals and procedures of representative democracy." But throughout time dissenting voices have appeared, some even proclaiming populism to be the only true form of democracy. Among the more recent defenders is Laclau, who believed that populism fosters a "democratization of democracy" by permitting the aggregation of demands of excluded sectors.

Both interpretations are to a certain extent correct. Depending on its electoral power and the context in which it arises, populism can work as *either* a threat to *or* a corrective for democracy. This means that populism per se is neither good nor bad for the democratic system. Just as other ideologies, such as liberalism, nationalism, or socialism, can have a positive and negative impact on democracy, so can populism. To better understand this complex relationship, we start by presenting a clear definition of democracy, which helps to clarify how the latter is positively and negatively affected by populist forces. We then present an original theoretical framework of the impact of populism on different political regimes, which allows us to distinguish the main effects of populism on the different stages of the *process* of both democratization and de-democratization.

Populism and (liberal) democracy

Just like populism, democracy is a highly contested concept in the academic realm and public space. The debates not only concern the correct definition of democracy, but also the various types of democracy. Although this is not the place to delve too deeply into this debate, we need to clarify our own understanding of democracy, before we can discuss its complex relationship with populism.

Democracy (*sans* adjectives) is best defined as the combination of popular sovereignty and majority rule; nothing more, nothing less. Hence, democracy can be direct or indirect, liberal or illiberal. In fact, the very etymology of the term *democracy* alludes to the idea of self-government of the people, i.e., a political system in which people rule. Not by chance, most "minimal" definitions consider democracy first and foremost as a *method* by which rulers are selected in competitive elections. Free and fair elections thus correspond to the defining property of democracy. Instead of changing rulers by violent conflict, the people agree that those who govern them should be elected by majority rule.

However, in most day-to-day usages the term *democracy* actually refers to *liberal* democracy rather than to democracy per se. The main difference between democracy (without adjectives) and liberal democracy is that the latter refers to a political regime, which not only respects popular sovereignty and majority rule, but also establishes independent institutions specialized in the protection of fundamental rights, such as freedom of expression and the protection of minorities. When it comes to protecting fundamental rights, there is no one-size-fits-all approach, and, in consequence, liberal democratic regimes have adopted very different institutional designs. For instance, some of them have a strong written constitution and Supreme Court (e.g., United States), while others have neither (e.g., United Kingdom). Despite these differences, *all* liberal democracies are characterized by institutions that aim to protect fundamental rights with the intention of avoiding the emergence of a "tyranny of the majority."

This interpretation is very close to the one proposed by the late U.S. political scientist Robert Dahl, who maintained that liberal democratic regimes are structured around two separate and independent dimensions: public contestation and political participation. While the former refers to the possibility to freely formulate preferences and oppose the government, the latter alludes to the right to participate in the political system. Moreover, to ensure the optimization of both dimensions, he believed a demanding set of so-called institutional guarantees is required, including freedom of expression, right to vote, eligibility for public office, alternative sources of information, among others.

Now that we have clear definitions of democracy and liberal democracy, it is time to reflect on how they are affected by populism. In short, populism is essentially democratic, but at odds with *liberal* democracy, the dominant model in the contemporary world. Populism holds that nothing should constrain "the will of the (pure) people" and fundamentally rejects the notions of pluralism and, therefore, minority rights as well as the "institutional guarantees" that should protect them.

In practice, populists often invoke the principle of popular sovereignty to criticize those independent institutions seeking to protect fundamental rights that are inherent to the liberal democratic model. Among the most targeted institutions are the judiciary and the media. For example, Berlusconi, who has been in and out of court for decades, would attack the judges for defending the interests of the Communists (hence, the term "Red Robes"). In pure populist fashion he once stated: "The government will continue to work, and parliament will make the necessary reforms to guarantee that a magistrate will not be able to try to illegitimately destroy someone who has been elected by the citizens." As expected, populists in power have often transformed the media landscape by turning state media into mouthpieces of the government and closing and harassing the few remaining independent media outlets. This has been the case, most recently, in Ecuador, Hungary, and Venezuela.

Populism exploits the tensions that are inherent to liberal democracy, which tries to find a harmonious equilibrium between majority rule and minority rights. This equilibrium is almost impossible to achieve in the real world, as the two overlap on important issues (think of antidiscrimination laws). Populists will criticize violations of the principle of majority rule as a breach of the very notion of democracy, arguing that ultimate political authority is vested in "the people" and not in unelected bodies. In essence, populism raises the question of who controls the controllers. As it tends to distrust any unelected institution that limits the power of the *demos*, populism can develop into a form of democratic extremism or, better said, of illiberal democracy.

In theory, populism is more negative for democracy in terms of public contestation and more positive in terms of political participation. On the one hand, populism tends to limit the scope of competition because it often maintains that those actors who are depicted as evil should be allowed to neither play the electoral game nor have access to the media. While it goes too far to call populism "the paranoid style of politics," populist forces are prone to highly charged rhetoric and conspiracy theories. For instance, Syriza politicians in Greece would refer to domestic opponents as "the fifth column" of Germany and one of its (now former) ministers even called the EU "terrorists." In the United States, a country in which some citizens are fascinated with conspiracy theories, many right-wing populists are convinced that elites among both Democrats and Republicans are working to establish a "new world government," which would put the United States under UN control.

On the other hand, populism tends to favor political participation, since it contributes to the mobilization of social groups who feel that their concerns are not being considered by the political establishment. As its core belief is that the people is sovereign, *all* the people and *only* the people should determine politics. It is worth noting that specific forms of populism, such as the populist radical right in Europe, might try to limit political participation by excluding certain minority groups. But these groups are excluded from the *native* people and not the *pure* people; in other words, it is the nativism and not the populism that is at the basis of the exclusion.

Table 1. Positive and negative effects of populism on liberal democracy

Positive effects	Negative effects
Populism can give voice to groups that do not feel represented by the political elite.	Populism can use the notion and praxis of majority rule to circumvent minority rights.
Populism can mobilize excluded sectors of society, improving their integration into the political system.	Populism can use the notion and praxis of popular sovereignty to erode the institutions specialized in the protection of fundamental rights.
Populism can improve the responsiveness of the political system, by fostering the implementation of policies preferred by excluded sectors of society.	Populism can promote the establishment of a new political cleavage, which impedes the formation of stable political coalitions.
Populism can increase democratic accountability, by making issues and policies part of the political realm.	Populism can lead to a moralization of politics whereby reaching agreements becomes extremely difficult if not impossible.

In summary, populism can play both a positive and a negative role for liberal democracy. For instance, by giving voice to constituencies that do not feel represented by the elite, populism works as a democratic corrective. Populists often do this by politicizing issues that are not discussed by the elites but are considered relevant by the "silent majority." Indeed, without the presence of populist radical right parties in Europe, immigration would probably not have become a significant topic for mainstream political parties in the 1990s. The same can be said about the economic and political integration of excluded sectors in contemporary Latin America. This topic has become one of the most pressing matters in the last decade, to a large extent due to the rise of left-wing populist presidents, such as Chávez in Venezuela and Morales in Bolivia, who successfully politicized the dramatic levels of inequality in their countries.

But populism can also have a negative impact on liberal democracy. For instance, by claiming that no institution has the right to constrain majority rule, populist forces can end up attacking minorities and eroding those institutions that specialize in the protection of fundamental rights. As a matter of fact, here lays the main threat posed by populist radical right parties to liberal democracy in Europe. Aiming to construct an ethnocracy, a model of democracy in which the state belongs to a single ethnic community, they undermine the rights of ethnic and religious minorities, such as Muslims in western Europe and Roma (gypsies) in eastern Europe.

Something similar occurs in contemporary Latin America, where left populist forces have drafted new constitutions that seriously diminish the capacity of the opposition to compete against the government for political power. A case in point is contemporary Ecuador, where President Correa has used constitutional reform not only to put loyal supporters in key state institutions, such as the electoral tribunal and the judiciary, but also to create new electoral districts and rules to favor his own

8. The Bolivarian government of Venezuela printed this stamp after the death of Hugo Chávez, a populist leader who was president of Venezuela from 1999 to 2013. Chávez wears the presidential sash, and crowds of his supporters assemble behind him.

political party. An almost identical process has recently taken place in Hungary.

Populism and the process of (de-)democratization

While a lively debate is ongoing on the role of populism in established liberal democracies, almost no attention is paid to the impact of populist forces on other political regimes and on the potential transition processes to either more or less democracy. What are the effects of populism on a (competitive) authoritarian regime or on fostering transformations toward more democracy? This is a blind spot that needs illumination.

Democracy is always incomplete and can at any time experience either deterioration or improvement. Therefore, it is important to think not only about *regimes* of (liberal) democracy, but also about *processes* of democratization (and de-democratization). Although there is no such thing as a "paradigmatic" democratization path, it is possible to recognize the existence of different episodes in which a movement toward either democratization or de-democratization occurs. Each of these stages alludes to the transition from one political regime to another, and we suggest that populism has a different effect in each. Let's begin by explaining the four most common political regimes in the contemporary world.

We can distinguish two different regimes within the authoritarian and the democratic camps, respectively: full authoritarianism and competitive authoritarianism, on the one hand, and electoral democracy and liberal democracy, on the other. In full authoritarianism there is no space for political opposition and there is systematic repression, while competitive authoritarianism does allow for limited contestation but within an uneven political playing field between incumbents and opposition. Competitive authoritarian regimes tolerate the presence of an opposition and conduct elections, but the latter are systematically violated in favor of officeholders.

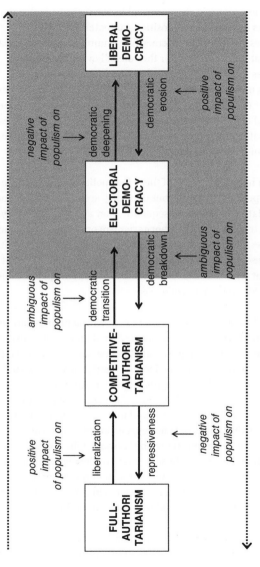

9. Populism can have positive and negative effects on different political regimes. In fact, populist forces can trigger episodes of institutional change that might well lead to both democratization and de-democratization.

Electoral democracy is characterized by the periodic realization of elections in which the opposition can potentially win. Nevertheless, electoral democracy has a number of institutional deficits that hinder respect for the rule of law and exhibit weaknesses in terms of independent institutions seeking the protection of fundamental rights. While liberal democracies are not perfect regimes, immune to accountability deficits, compared to electoral democracies the governed have more opportunities to hold the authorities accountable, ranging from a robust public sphere to independent judicial oversight.

It is worth noting that each of these four political regimes have their own political dynamic, but once they are in place they tend to remain relatively stable. Consequently, they are not *necessarily* in transition toward (more) authoritarianism or (more) democracy. Nevertheless, the rise of populist forces can trigger changes within each of these regimes. We theorize about the particular kind of impact that populism has on each of the transition episodes and illustrate this on the basis of one case each.

The impact of populism on the democratization process can be divided into three episodes: liberalization, democratic transition, and democratic deepening. During the first stage of *liberalization*, when an authoritarian regime loosens restrictions and expands some individual and group rights, populism tends to be *grosso modo*, a positive force for democracy. Because it helps articulate demands of popular sovereignty and majority rule, which call into question existing forms of state repression, populism contributes to the formation of a "master frame" through which opposition leaders can mobilize (all) those opposed to the regime. A good example of this can be found in the role that populism played in some of the broad opposition movements in communist eastern Europe, most notably the Solidarity trade union in Poland.

Solidarity was an anticommunist umbrella organization, harboring a broad and loose coalition of actors who agreed on the problem of the communist present almost as much as they disagreed on the preferred post-communist future. While Solidarity as such was not a populist movement, some leaders and constituencies of the movement adhered to populism, which was particularly expressed at mass demonstrations by its iconic leader Lech Walesa. Fundamentally, Solidarity represented "the people" against "the elite" of the Polish United Workers Party (PZSR) in both ethnic (nationalist) and moral (populist) terms. It is not a coincidence that (leading) members of the Solidarity movement would found various populist parties in the post-communist period, of which the most notable is the right-wing populist Law and Justice (PiS) party of twin brothers Lech and Jarosław Kaczyńsky.

In the stage of *democratic transition*, i.e., the transition from a competitive (or fully) authoritarian regime to an electoral democracy, populism plays an ambiguous, but still rather constructive role, fostering the idea that the people should elect their rulers. Given that populist forces are characterized by claiming that politics is about respecting popular sovereignty at any cost, they will attack the elites in power and push for a change in the form through which access to political power is warranted. This means that they will support the realization of free and fair elections. An interesting case in this regard is Cuauhtémoc Cárdenas in Mexico and the formation of the Party of the Democratic Revolution (PRD) at the end of the 1980s.

The PRD split from the Institutional Revolutionary Party (PRI), which—under a succession of names—had been in power since 1929 and, despite its democratic façade, ruled a competitive authoritarian regime. Once Cárdenas and others realized that it was not possible to change the neoliberal economic policies of the PRI from within, they opted to build a new political vehicle that would not only oppose neoliberalism, but also demand the full implementation of free and fair elections. Since its beginning, the PRD adopted a populist language in order to present its party leader—initially Cárdenas and later Andrés Manuel López Obrador (AMLO)—as a "humble man of the people," interested in building a real democracy for all Mexicans. Although the PRD was not able to win the presidency itself, it did help pave the way for the historic deals that enabled the "founding elections" of 2000, in which the conservative National Action Party (PAN) won the presidency.

Finally, during the stage of *democratic deepening*, pending reforms that are crucial for improving institutions specialized in the protection of fundamental rights and the development of a fully-fledged liberal democratic regime are completed. Theoretically, populists are at odds with the process of democratic deepening, as they support an interpretation of democracy based on unconstrained popular will and the rejection of unelected bodies. The latter are normally portrayed by populism as illegitimate institutions, which seek to defend the "special interests" of powerful minorities rather than the "real" interests of the people.

Three-time Slovak prime minister Vladimír Mečiar provides an excellent example of populist opposition to democratic deepening, particularly during his third and last coalition government (1994–1998), which consisted of three populist parties. When Mečiar came to power in 1994, Slovakia was in the group of democratic frontrunners for accession to the European Union (EU) in post-communist central and eastern Europe. As a consequence of the government's illiberal politics, which included both disregard for laws as well as (attempted) efforts to change laws—such as the redrawing of electoral districts to undermine the opposition parties—the country slowly but steadily retreated into the category of democratic laggards. The EU even threatened to exclude Slovakia from the first round of accession.

The last decades have served as a reminder that democracy can be not only deepened, but also diluted, and even abolished. Populism can play a significant role in this process of de-democratization too, which can also be divided in three episodes: democratic erosion, democratic breakdown, and repressiveness. The stage of *democratic erosion* includes incremental changes to undermine the autonomy of those institutions that specialize in the protection of fundamental rights, such as diminishing judiciary independency, jettisoning the rule of law, and weakening minority rights. Populist leaders and followers are inclined to trigger episodes of democratic erosion because they support, in essence, an extreme majoritarian model of democracy that opposes any groups or institutions that stand in the way of implementing "the general will of the people." Probably no better illustration of the ways in which populism can lead to a process of democratic erosion can be cited than the current situation in Hungary.

After losing the 2002 elections, a loss he only grudgingly acknowledged, Viktor Orbán and his right-wing populist Fidesz party adopted a radical opposition outlook that even included violent street protests. Upon his return to power in 2010, he used his party's electoral majority to force through a new constitution that ensures, in the words of some academic observers, that "(t)he current government now has very few checks on its own power, but the new constitutional order permits the governing party to lodge its loyalists in crucial long-term positions with veto power over what future governments might do." Although foreign governments and international organizations have been reluctant to criticize the Orbán government too harshly, both the EU and the United States have expressed growing concerns with the "crackdown" on democracy in Hungary.

The second stage in the process of de-democratization is *democratic breakdown*, denoting a regime shift from electoral democracy to competitive authoritarianism (or full authoritarianism in an extreme case). Populist actors are expected to play an ambiguous, but still rather supportive role during democratic breakdown, because they are inclined to tilt the rules of the game in favor of populist forces and/or attack "the corrupt elite" for not permitting the expression of the general will of the people. Fujimori's regime in Peru is a case in point.

Fujimori came to power as a populist outsider in 1990, campaigning against the political establishment and in favor of a gradual approach to solve the economic crisis that the country was facing. Given that Fujimori neither had a strong party behind him nor was interested in establishing alliances with the existing parties, the country experienced a real deadlock between the executive and legislative powers. To break the deadlock, Fujimori suspended the constitution and closed the parliament in 1992, arguing that he was simply following "the will of the people." After this *autogolpe* (self-coup), Peru continued to be governed by Fujimori for eight more years, during which the regime was certainly closer to competitive authoritarianism than to electoral democracy. In fact, Fujimori established an alliance with military sectors—in particular with the intelligence service and its director Vladimiro Montesinos—with the aim of not only destroying the Shining Path guerrilla movement, but also skewing the playing field to the disadvantage of the opposition.

Finally, the last stage of de-democratization is *repressiveness*, the movement from a competitive authoritarian to a full authoritarian regime, a process that usually unfolds gradually and is related to the occurrence of crises. Given that populism inherently supports popular sovereignty and majority rule, we believe that populists will generally oppose this process of repressiveness. There are almost no recent cases of repressiveness, in which a populist actor has been relevant.

One of the few exceptions is probably Belarusian president Aleksandr Lukashenka, who—despite opportunity and rising opposition—has not transformed his competitive authoritarian regime into a fully authoritarian one. The main reason that Lukashenka has supported a competitive authoritarian regime, based on (increasingly rigged) electoral support, rather than the fully authoritarian "clan politics" of other post-Soviet countries, is his populist ideology. He justifies his (competitive authoritarian) regime on the basis of a populist argumentation, in which the opposition is painted as a "corrupt elite," aligned to foreign (i.e., Western) powers. However, for Lukashenka to be able to claim to be the true representative of "the pure Belarusian people" with some legitimacy, he needs a popular contest with his opponents, even if it is through elections that are not truly competitive.

Intervening variables

This theoretical framework distinguishes, first and foremost, between the effects of populism in the six distinct stages of the processes of democratization and de-democratization. However, within each stage the nature and strength of the effect can vary too, depending on at least three intervening variables: the political power of populist forces, the type of political system in which populist actors operate, and the international context.

The most important factor is the political power of the populist actor. Whether populist forces are in opposition or in government can affect not only the strength, but also the nature of their impact on the process of democratization. In general, populists-in-opposition tend to call for more transparency and the implementation of more democracy (e.g., founding elections, referendums, recall votes) to break the alleged stranglehold of the elite, either in a (competitive) authoritarian or in an (electoral) democratic context.

Populists-in-power have a more complicated relationship with the use of direct democracy and respect of the rules of public contestation. Although it is true that populists defend majority rule, only some of them have more or less consistently used plebiscitary instruments. Most notably, Chávez organized several referendums, including a successful one to overturn term limits for the presidency, which allowed him to win reelection for the second time, and an unsuccessful one to change the constitution. Populist politicians have also used their political power to tilt the electoral playing field in their own favor, as both Correa and Orbán have done through constitutional reforms.

A second important factor is the *type* of political system. Like all political actors, once populists come to power in a democratic system they are more or less constrained by the specific features of the political regime in which they operate. While presidential systems make it easier for populist "outsiders" to gain power, they often lack support at other levels to push through their agenda—particularly when they lack a strong party organization. In contrast, parliamentary systems tend to limit the power of populists-in-power because they often lead to coalition governments, in which populist parties have to work together with mostly stronger nonpopulist parties—as was the case with the FPÖ in Austria, for example. However, if a populist actor, or coalition of actors, acquires a parliamentary majority, they have fewer counterbalancing forces to contend with—as is most strikingly illustrated by Hungary, where Orbán for a long time could count on a qualified parliamentary majority, allowing him to change the constitution without any impedimentary action by the opposition.

Finally, the international context plays an important role. If a country is integrated into a strong network of liberal democracies, such as the EU, it is more difficult, but not impossible (again, see Hungary under Orbán), for a populist actor to undermine key features of liberal democracy without a major international backlash. Not by chance, the recent coming to power of left populist governments in various Latin American countries has been accompanied by efforts to construct new regional institutions, such as the Union of South American Nations (UNASUR), which are trying to defend their own model of democracy. In fact, UNASUR has developed its own system of electoral observation to compete with the system of the

Organization of American States (OAS), the main intercontinental organization in the Americas, in which Canada and the United States are also member states.

Populism and democracy revisited

The complexity of the relationship between populism and democracy is reflected in theory and practice. In essence, populism is not against democracy; rather it is at odds with *liberal* democracy. It is a set of ideas that defends extreme majoritarianism and supports a form of illiberal democracy. Populism strongly champions popular sovereignty and majority rule but opposes minority rights and pluralism. But even its relationship with liberal democracy is not one-sided. Around the world populist forces seek to give voice and power to marginalized groups, but they also tend to combat the very existence of oppositional forces and transgress the rules of political competition.

In practice, populists usually cite and exploit a tension inherent in many liberal democracies of the contemporary world: they criticize the poor *results* of the democratic regime, and, to solve this problem, they campaign for a modification of the democratic *procedures*. When the liberal democratic regime does not deliver what certain constituencies want, political entrepreneurs can adopt the populist set of ideas to criticize the establishment and argue that the time has come to strengthen popular sovereignty. Put another way, populists tend to claim that the rule of law and the institutions in charge of the protection of fundamental rights (e.g., electoral tribunals, constitutional courts, supreme courts, etc.) not only limit the capacity of the people to exercise their rightful power, but also give rise to growing discontent with the political system.

Populism does not have the same effect in each stage of the democratization process. In fact, we suggest that populism tends to play a positive role in the promotion of an electoral or minimal democracy, but a negative role when it comes to fostering the development of a full-fledged liberal democratic regime. Consequently, while populism tends to favor the democratization of authoritarian regimes, it is prone to diminish the quality of liberal democracies. Populism supports popular sovereignty, but it is inclined to oppose any limitations on majority rule, such as judicial independence and minority rights. Populism-in-power has led to processes of de-democratization (e.g., Orbán in Hungary or Chávez in Venezuela) and, in some extreme cases, even to the breakdown of the democratic regime (e.g., Fujimori in Peru).

If the democratic system becomes stable, populists will continue to challenge any limitations on majority rule, and when they become strong enough, they can cause a process of democratic erosion. However, it is unlikely that they will threaten the existence of the democratic system to the point of producing its breakdown, as they will experience strong resistance from multiple actors and institutions that defend the existence of independent bodies specialized in the protection of fundamental rights. To a certain extent, this is the scenario that some European countries are experiencing today, in which populist forces have become electorally dominant (e.g., Greece or Hungary) but do not have absolute leeway to revamp the whole institutional design of their countries.

Chapter 6
Causes and responses

Despite the vibrant debate about populism, surprisingly few established theories about the success (and failure) of populist forces exist. Most explanations of populist success emphasize the appearance of a charismatic leader, who is able to attract a readily available part of the electorate that is disappointed in or feels ignored by the mainstream political parties. This interpretation is problematic for at least two reasons. First, not all successful populist actors are led by a charismatic leader. Second, populism is a moral and Manichean discourse that exists in society regardless of the presence of populist actors. Whether one likes it or not, many citizens interpret political reality through the lens of populism.

To explain the success (and failure) of populist actors one has to take into account both the demand side and the supply side of populist politics. One of the major advantages of the ideational approach is that it accommodates for populism at both the elite and the mass level. Societies with strong demand for populism represent a fertile soil for success, but they still require the supply of credible populist forces. At the same time, a strong supply of populism without a comparable demand will often lead to the failure of populist actors. In addition, to understand the rise of populism it is crucial to consider the ways in which the socioeconomic and sociopolitical context can both hinder and facilitate the demand for and supply of populism.

After discussing the main factors for the success and failure of populism, we will address another important but elusive issue: how to respond to the rise of populism? To answer this question, we map different democratic responses that target the demand side and the supply side of populist politics. We end this book with some suggestions on how best to both strengthen populism's positive effects and weaken its negative effects on (liberal) democracy.

Explaining success and failure of populism

Let's begin with a brief clarification. While it is true that the success of political actors is normally measured by the number of votes they obtain (electoral strength), political success can be analyzed in at least two other ways: the ability to put topics on the public agenda (agenda-setting) and the capacity to shape public policies (policy impact). This distinction is particularly relevant when we think about the success and failure of populist actors. After all, in many places in the world populists attract a fairly limited number of votes, but, nevertheless, they play a notable role in terms of agenda-setting and policy impact. There is no better example of this than populist radical right parties like the Danish People's Party (DF) and the French National Front (FN) in western Europe. Although these parties gain "only" between 10 and 20 percent of the vote in national elections, they have been influential in putting issues like immigration and multiculturalism at the center of the public debate. In some cases they have even forced mainstream parties to adopt more restrictive asylum and immigration policies.

Irrespective of the type of political success, populist actors can thrive only when elite and mass populism come together. As a consequence, a theory that seeks to explain the success (and failure) of populism must consider both the demand side and the supply side of populist politics. While the former alludes to occasional and structural changes contributing to the rise of populist attitudes and the salience of the populist set of ideas, the latter refers to conditions favoring the performance of populist forces in the political arena.

The demand side of populist politics

For any political actor to be successful, there has to be a demand for her message. Most populist actors combine populism with one or more so-called host ideologies, such as some form of nationalism or socialism. Although populism is often noted as a reason for their success, many electoral studies instead focus exclusively on the accompanying features, such as xenophobia in western Europe or socioeconomic support for disadvantaged groups in Latin America. This is in part a consequence of the lack of available data at the mass level. Empirical studies of populist attitudes are still in their infancy, but they do show that populist attitudes are quite widespread among populations in countries with relevant populist parties (e.g., Netherlands) and social movements (e.g., the United States) as well as in countries with no relevant populist actors (e.g., Chile).

Significant parts of populations around the world support important aspects of the populist set of ideas. Most notably, many people think that the (political) establishment is dishonest and self-serving, makes corrupt deals behind closed doors, and does not care about the opinions of the majority. Many believe that "the people" should take the most important decisions instead of delegating its sovereign power to professional politicians. This notwithstanding, populist attitudes are often latent, i.e., lying dormant or hidden until circumstances are suitable for their development or manifestation. In the words of U.S. populism scholar Kirk Hawkins: 'There is a dormant Hugo Chávez or Sarah Palin inside all of us. The question is how does he or she get activated?'

This is where the socioeconomic and sociopolitical context comes in. Demand for populism manifests itself under specific (sets of) circumstances. It is set in motion when the perception is widespread that threats to the very existence of society are present. This is why major policy failures, such as dramatic economic downturns and, above all, disclosures of cases of systematic corruption can work as a catalyst for populist attitudes among the population. By way of illustration, without the Great Recession and the corrupt behavior of the mainstream parties it is difficult to understand the sharp rise in public support for populist parties such as Podemos in Spain and Syriza in Greece, whereas without the so-called *Tangentopoli* corruption scandal in Italy at the beginning of the 1990s it is impossible to comprehend the rise of Silvio Berlusconi.

Corruption scandals show that individuals and groups of "the elite" behave in a dishonest manner. It makes people angry about

10. Alexis Tsipras (left) and Pablo Iglesias (right) are the leaders of two leftist populist parties (Syriza in Greece and Podemos in Spain, respectively) who have generated both admiration and anxiety across Europe. They are young politicians who have garnered respect for their efforts to combat austerity after the onset of the Great Recession.

the political situation and susceptible to interpreting political reality through the lens of populism. Systemic corruption thrives especially in countries with serious problems of "stateness," i.e., the capacity of the state to alter the existing distribution of resources, activities, and interpersonal connections. Weak states have difficulties collecting taxes from citizens (resources), controlling criminal groups (activities), and interfering with existing patrimonial networks (interpersonal connections). Democratic regimes with serious stateness problems are prone to suffer systemic corruption, which can lead to endemic populism (e.g., Ecuador and Greece) or continuous struggle between populist and nonpopulist forces (e.g., Argentina and Slovakia). Importantly, the coming into power of populists does not necessarily lead to a stronger state or the ability to tackle the roots of the stateness problem.

Another key factor in the activation of populist attitudes is the general feeling that the political system is unresponsive. When citizens feel that the political parties and governments do not listen to them and ignore their demands, the possibility grows that populism becomes active, at least within the constituencies that feel abandoned by the establishment. Once voters feel orphaned by the established political actors, they become inclined to interpret political events through the mental map of populism: "the elite only cares about themselves and are not interested in the concerns of the (real) people." It is no coincidence that a significant part of the electorate of populist radical right parties in Europe consists of the "native" working class, which no longer feels represented by social democratic parties that have embraced economic globalization, European integration, and multiculturalism.

One of the key reasons for the growing gap between the elite and the people was aptly noted by the late Irish political scientist Peter Mair, who argued that mainstream political parties increasingly face tension between their roles as suitable representatives and responsible agents. Citizens often want their representatives to do one thing, while they have a responsibility to do something else. This is particularly true in contemporary Europe, where the European Union (EU) has significantly diminished the room for maneuver of national governments, sometimes even forcing them to implement policies they openly oppose.

For instance, because of the pressures of international markets and the EU, the social democratic governments of José Luis Rodríguez Zapatero in Spain (2004–2011) and Georgios Papandreou in Greece (2009–2011) decided to act as "responsible agents" by enacting austerity reforms, generating frustration among many voters who felt betrayed and no longer represented by their party. This contributed to the activation of populist sentiments, which were channeled first through social movements like the *Indignados* and then by left populist parties like Podemos and Syriza. Although this is an extreme example, established political parties in the EU are compelled to strike an increasingly difficult balance between responsiveness and responsibility. The better they are able to deal with this challenge, which includes being honest about this tension among the voters, the lesser the chances that populism will thrive.

Something similar has occurred in Latin America, where the policy options of national governments are heavily constrained by international markets and international financial institutions like the International Monetary Fund (IMF) and the World Bank. An extreme example of this "perfect storm" is the socioeconomic and sociopolitical situation that facilitated the rise of Hugo Chávez in Venezuela. Falling oil prices in the last two decades of the previous century led to an absence of money and to growing public debt, undermining the country's two-party system that was heavily dependent on clientelist networks. When center-left president Carlos Andrés Pérez implemented austerity reforms, he faced major social revolts as well as a coup d'état by a young lieutenant colonel named Hugo Chávez. When Pérez was forced out of office by the Supreme Court, due to a corruption scandal, the political establishment became increasingly discredited and, once released from prison, Chávez mobilized this resentment with a strong populist discourse attacking the elite (*la oligarquía*) and glorifying the people (*el pueblo*). In 1998 Chávez won the presidential election with 56 percent of the vote, marking the collapse of the traditional two-party system of the country and the beginning of the third populist era in Latin American history.

When analyzing the rise of populism, it is worth indicating that subtle and long-term changes of contemporary societies can facilitate not only the diffusion, but also the activation of populist attitudes. U.S. political scientist Ronald Inglehart has argued that the social transformation of postwar Western democracies has created a process of "cognitive mobilization" among its populations, who have become better informed, more independent, and more self-conscious. This new emancipated citizen no longer accepts the natural dominance of the political elites and strongly criticizes any alleged wrongdoings. Moreover, the emancipated citizen is much more aware of the alleged wrongdoings of the political elites because of the new information environment in which she operates.

First of all, the traditional media is less controlled by the political elites. In many countries newspapers were initially strongly linked, if not fully owned and operated, by established political parties or organizations, while radio and television were exclusively owned and controlled by the state, which meant that they were either pro-governmental parties or pro-mainstream parties (including the established opposition parties). Today most newspapers are more or less independent from political parties, while state radio and television have lost much of their audience to commercial competitors. They all have to compete with an ever-growing number of online media sources. In this incredibly competitive market, media organizations have decreased their focus on serious political issues and increased their coverage of issues that sell, such as crime and corruption, staples of the populist diet. All this has created a political culture that is not necessarily populist as such, but one that is definitely more conducive to populist messages.

While the process of cognitive mobilization has been more limited in developing countries, often reaching mainly urban middle classes, traditional institutions and values are losing power around the world. Moreover, the ascendance of social media has been profound in developing countries as well, be they democratic or authoritarian. The combination of these changes can be seen in both the Green Revolution in Iran and the Arab Spring in the broader Middle East, which provide powerful examples of the ability to mobilize empowered urban middle classes using social media. If democratic aspirations and anti-establishment sentiments come together, particularly among large discriminated social groups, (proto-)populist sentiments will be activated.

The supply side of populist politics

Most populist episodes are linked to the rise (and fall) of a populist leader or party. It is this populist actor who is able to exploit the existing context to mobilize the amorphous anti-establishment sentiments and to appeal to the population by promoting "common sense" solutions. Successful populists are able to combine a broad range of societal grievances around a populist discourse of "us, the good people" against "them, the corrupt elite." They do this by attaching their populism to host ideologies, which address other key aspects of these societal grievances. For instance, contemporary populist radical right parties in western Europe connect nativism and populism when accusing the corrupt (native) elite of favoring the (alien) immigrants and marginalizing the (native) people. Similarly, left-wing populists in South America combine socialism and populism to accuse the corrupt elite of plundering the country's natural resources at the expense of the poor people.

Independent of the existing socioeconomic and sociopolitical context, populist actors try to politicize issues that are not being (adequately) addressed by the establishment. When mainstream political parties converge, and few significant differences remain between their programmatic platforms, it becomes easier for populist forces to argue that "they" are all the same. The FN was the first to successfully develop this discourse in Europe, referring to the four mainstream parties as the "Gang of Four," which, through a secret pact, had "confiscated democracy." Later the party began to refer to the two remaining established parties as one, merging their abbreviations UMP and PS into "UMPS." In Italy the comedian-turned-politician Beppe Grillo, leader of the populist Five Star Movement (M5S), refers to the center left PD as 'PdminusL' (*Pdmenoelle*), arguing that it is indistinguishable from the center right PdL.

Of course, mainstream political parties often provide a response of their own to the ideological convergence. Realizing that certain issues are relevant to the electorate, they choose to politicize them. By doing so, they not only challenge their established competitors, but also close the space for new challengers, including populist forces. In other words, both the actions *and* inactions of mainstream political parties play a major role in the success and failure of populist forces. This can be illustrated with a comparison of the electoral performance of populist radical right parties in Austria and Spain.

Spain is one of the few western European countries without a relevant populist radical right party. In addition to the presence of strong regional parties and a very peculiar electoral system, a major explanation is that the Popular Party (PP), the mainstream right-wing party, has addressed many of the issues that potential voters for populist radical right parties in Spain care about: Catholicism, law and order, and above all national unity. In sharp contrast, the Freedom Party of Austria (FPÖ) profited heavily from the convergence of the two main parties, which often formed a formal or informal grand coalition to govern the country and keep potentially divisive issues, such as European integration and immigration, off the political and public agenda.

But populist actors are not just hapless products of their environments. They are actively involved in creating a more fertile breeding ground themselves. Most notably, populists spare no effort in creating *a sense of* crisis. Often nonintentionally helped by sensationalist media, populist radical right parties in Europe try to redefine (sometimes relatively modest) increases in refugees as an "immigration crisis," which they contend is caused by the incompetent and corrupt mainstream parties. In other words, whether populist actors become successful in terms of electoral strength, agenda-setting, or policy impact is strongly related to their ability to develop a credible narrative of crisis. This is important for another reason as well: by creating a sense of crisis, populists inject urgency and importance to their message.

A good example is provided by Finland, which experienced an important contraction in gross domestic product but only a moderate increase in unemployment and sovereign debt in the first years of the Great Recession. It would therefore be a strong exaggeration to say that the average Finnish voter was hard hit by the global economic crisis. This notwithstanding, the populist True Finns party obtained an astonishing 19 percent of the vote in the 2011 parliamentary elections. While helped by a corruption scandal that affected all major parties, the sense of crisis created by the party, and by parts of the media, played a decisive role in its success. Claiming that their generous welfare state was threatened by the EU bailout programs and by an "invasion" of immigrants, both permitted by the mainstream parties, the True Finns claimed that "the innocent" (read: the people) were made to pay for the silliness of "the guilty" (read: the elite).

Before moving to the next section, it is important to address an oft-forgotten but nevertheless important question: how does political culture influence the potential emergence of populism? Populist actors do not operate in a vacuum; rather, they emerge in societies with historical legacies that give rise to different political cultures. Take, for instance, the case of the western European democratization processes, which often took hundreds of years to develop and were strongly elite-controlled. It pitted nondemocratic elitists, such as the monarchy and landowners, against democratic elitists, notably liberals and socialists. Indeed, the liberal and socialist elites tended to be deeply distrustful of "the common people," which is why they extended suffrage only incrementally and grudgingly (including to women). Moreover, the rise of communism and fascism strengthened this distrust of the (common) people, leading democratic elites in many countries to constrain the choice of political options; for instance, many countries prohibited "anti-democratic" parties so that the people would not be able to make the "wrong choice" again.

In sharp contrast, the United States has a more popular democratic history, which is characterized by a revolutionary rhetoric and the very notion of "we, the people." Ironically, many of the Founding Fathers actually had deep reservations towards what President Lincoln would famously describe as "government of the people, by the people, for the people." In fact, the extremely complex and quite dysfunctional political system created by the nation's founders reflected both their anti-elite and anti-people sentiments, as can be seen from the checks and balances they put in place and the Electoral College they established, respectively. This notwithstanding, American political culture has always been strongly populist, pitting the pure people against the elite or, in contemporary campaign discourse, Main Street versus Wall Street. The idea that the people are virtuous and the elite corrupt has been propagated in both high and low culture throughout the history of the United States.

Even without the intervention of populist leaders or parties, Americans meet with populist discourse in the mainstream media and from mainstream politicians. Moreover, populist sentiments play a major role in popular culture as well. From Thomas Paine's famous pamphlet *Common Sense* (1776) through the epic movie *Mr. Smith Goes to Washington* (1939), starring James Stewart, to John Rich's more recent anti-bailout country song "Shuttin' Detroit Down" (2009), Americans are told about the eternal struggle between the pure people and the corrupt elite.

Given the historical legacies it is not surprising that populism has been relatively rare in western European history, limited to top-down mobilization by flash parties like the Poujadists. But the social transformation of the "silent revolution" has made western European cultures more open to populism. The emancipated citizens have freed themselves from the control of the traditional political and social organizations and have grown increasingly critical, not to say cynical, toward the establishment. As the elite is increasingly seen in a bad light, the people have transformed from predominantly bad to primarily good. Many media have ditched the (academic) expert for "the man in the street" in their coverage of important political developments. Mainstream politicians are badgered in interviews, having to respond to the "concerns of the people," often with the journalist as the voice of the people. Related, reality television programs featuring ordinary people, like *Big Brother*, or "low culture" celebrities, like the Kardashians, have largely replaced shows about the lives of the "high culture" elites.

Responses against populism

Although the electoral successes of populists were initially concentrated mainly in Latin America, populist forces have been establishing themselves in electoral arenas around the world in the past decades. This has led to growing concerns and debates about the best way to deal with them. Much of this debate is influenced by the concept of *militant democracy*, a term coined by the German philosopher and political scientist Karl Löwenstein, who, in the 1930s, argued that democracies should ban extremist political forces to prevent them from coming to power by democratic means—as he himself had experienced with the rise of Adolf Hitler in Weimar Germany. Although Germany is one of the few countries to officially define itself as a militant democracy in its constitution, most democracies have implemented at least some of its features—and even more since the terrorist attacks of 9/11 and the subsequent War on Terror.

When it comes to dealing with populist forces, the militant democracy approach is particularly problematic though, since populism is not against democracy per se but rather at odds with the *liberal* democratic regime. Populist forces are suspicious about the very existence of unelected institutions, not always without reason, that can run amok and end up protecting the interests of powerful minorities rather than upholding the common good. This means that populists present a different, more complex, challenge to democracies than extremists and, therefore, require a different, more complex, response. In fact, overreacting to the populist challenge can do more harm than good to liberal democracy.

Demand side responses

How to cope with the demand for populist politics is rarely addressed in academic or public debates. This is partly because many people reduce populism to an elite-driven process, centered on charismatic leaders, who have the ability to enchant (or "trick") the masses. In this understanding, populism is explained by the rise of "great men" like Jörg Haider or Hugo Chávez. However, populist attitudes are relatively widespread in societies, even in those without a charismatic populist leader. Their activation depends on the presence of specific sets of conditions, under which ordinary people might become fervent populists, most notably political corruption in general and elite unresponsiveness in particular.

11. Much of the electoral success of the Austrian Freedom Party can be attributed to Jörg Haider's charismatic figure. He was a talented speaker who spared no effort in using populist ideas to attack the establishment and politicize the issue of immigration.

Major corruption scandals and particularly systemic corruption create fertile breeding grounds for populism among important swaths of the population. Consequently, fighting and preventing corruption are crucial strategies for diminishing the demand side of populist politics. The first lesson to be drawn from this is that, once a major corruption scandal comes to light, the worst thing to do is to deny it or avoid a proper transparent investigation. An important part of the legitimacy of *liberal* democracy comes precisely from the existence of autonomous institutions, which are able to hold state officials and elected politicians accountable to the citizens. Adequate prosecution and sanctioning of major cases of corruption does not only reduce the occurrence of corruption among the elites, but also shows to the people that "the system" is not fully controlled by one homogeneous establishment.

Dealing with systemic corruption is undoubtedly much more challenging than coping with single cases of major corruption. After all, systemic corruption often accompanies problems of "stateness" and confronting this is anything but easy. Efforts to strengthen state capacity in general, and the rule of law in particular, should be seen as measures that indirectly contribute to weakening populist sentiments. The stronger the capacity of the state to alter the existing distribution of resources, activities, and interpersonal connections, the higher the odds that the demand for populism stays dormant. Therefore, international organizations and governmental institutions that are involved in "democracy promotion" should use carrot-and-stick measures to build state capacity and the rule of law. A common "carrot" measure consists of improving the working conditions of state employees and encouraging citizens to report wrongdoings (e.g., ombudsman), "stick" measures are normally related to institutional and legal reforms seeking to enhance the oversight and sanction of state agents.

However, most western European countries do not suffer serious problems of stateness and yet face widespread populism at the mass level. For instance, Denmark and the Netherlands have seen the emergence of strong populist parties even though neither systemic corruption nor state capacity is a fundamental problem in the country. To understand this, it is important to consider the second condition that facilitates the activation of populist sentiments among the population: elite unresponsiveness. In many western European countries the established parties have prioritized responsibility over representation and have countered the consequent loss of public support by forming political cartels, often with the explicit argument to keep populist parties out of power. Obviously, this is a dream come true for the populists, as it confirms their preferred image of fighting a struggle of "one against all, all against one"—an old slogan of the populist radical right party Flemish Bloc (now Flemish Interest, VB) in Belgium.

The main problem is not necessarily that established parties form cartels with other liberal democratic parties, or that they act responsibly, but that they are not clear and honest about it. Most politicians claim full agency when things go well and almost full lack of agency when things go wrong. For example, economic growth is claimed as a success of the government's economic policies, while an economic downturn is externalized as a consequence of "globalization" and international institutions like the EU and the IMF. Essentially, politicians set themselves up for failure by claiming to have more power than they really have. As they cannot change the fundamental restrictions to their power, they should be more open about them, which includes explaining why they accept the restrictions. This would still leave space for populists to present a potentially more attractive story, i.e., of full sovereignty, but it would at least make the mainstream parties look less deceiving and more genuine. In addition, recent experiences in countries like Greece, where the left populist Syriza government had to succumb to the same economic reality as its "treacherous" opponents before it, have taken away some of the allure of the populist alternative.

Before moving to the next section, it is worth indicating that to cope with the demand side of populist politics one can also think about active strategies targeted at the mass level. One of the most important is civic education, which is aimed at socializing the citizenry into the main values of liberal democracy and, although not always openly, warning about the dangers of extremist challengers. Probably the most elaborate civic education program exists in Germany, which even has a separate government agency charged with carrying it out—the somewhat ominously termed Federal Office for Civic Education (BpB). Overall, civic education can strengthen democratic beliefs and explain the relevance of pluralism, which can play an important role in preventing populist attitudes. Strong warnings against extremist forces can backfire, however, particularly among groups who are already more distrustful of the political establishment and more sympathetic to populist actors.

Supply side responses

Because populist forces are prone to attack the establishment, the latter often reacts against them. While some democratic responses are directed at diminishing the demand for populist politics, most actions and actors target exclusively the supply of populist politics, i.e., the populist actors. Still, contrary to the populist discourse, the establishment is not a monolithic entity and some of its actors are more willing to respond to populism and successful in doing so. We focus on the following four establishment actors, which tend to be the most active and effective: (1) mainstream political actors, (2) institutions specialized in the protection of fundamental rights, (3) the media, and (4) supranational institutions.

Mainstream political actors and populist actors are essentially in the same business: politics. Consequently, under certain circumstances they can decide to cooperate and generate an alliance, which can help them increase the visibility of their demands and acquire political power. For instance, mainstream political parties in European countries such as Austria and Finland have formed government coalitions with populist parties, while in the United States several leaders of the Republican Party have established a formal or informal alliance with populist Tea Party groups to win seats in Congress. Most mainstream political parties take the opposite direction, however, and openly attack populist actors. One way of doing this is by ostracizing populists, for example by constructing a so-called *cordon sanitaire* around them that excludes any official collaboration—this has been the case, most notably, in Belgium with regard to the VB. A more radical approach is to fight populist forces by all available means, including a general strike or even a putsch against populists in power—as happened in Venezuela at the beginning of the 2000s.

Institutions specialized in the protection of fundamental rights can play a crucial role when it comes to dealing with the rise of populists. After all, in liberal democracies, institutions such as the German Federal Constitutional Court and the U.S. Supreme Court are specifically designed to safeguard the liberal democratic system and to protect minority rights against majority rule. In central and eastern Europe the judiciary has often been the most important counterweight to populist actors, opposing some of the more illiberal proposals of populists such as the Kaczyński brothers in Poland and Mečiar in Slovakia. However, it does not always work. For instance, the judiciary possessed insufficient power to prevent illiberal constitutional reforms under Correa in Ecuador and under Orbán in Hungary, which enabled these populist leaders to concentrate power and put loyal supporters in the legal apparatus.

The media play an important part in the political failure and success of populist forces. For instance, without the support of high-profile personalities on Fox News and several local radio stations, such as Glenn Beck and Sean Hannity, it is difficult to understand the rise of the Tea Party. Something similar occurred in Austria, where FPÖ leader Haider profited from very favorable coverage of the main tabloid, *Die Krone*, in the 1990s. More recently the United Kingdom Independence Party (UKIP) has profited from the open support of the British tabloid *Daily Express*, which had earlier backed Labour and the Conservatives. In some cases the populist actor is a (social) media personality, launching his or her political career in the media—as was the case with Attack leader Volen Sidorov in Bulgaria and M5S leader Beppe Grillo in Italy. The quintessential case of this type of media populism is Berlusconi, who used his vast media empire to launch his Forza Italia party and to support him in office.

Quite different is the situation in Germany, where the media has been very hostile to populist parties of the right and left. Even a tabloid like *Bild*, which disseminates a strong populist discourse itself, vehemently attacks parties like the left populist The Left (Die Linke) and the right populist The Republicans (Die Republikaner).

A similar situation exists in the United Kingdom, despite the recent switch in support of the *Daily Express*. For example, all tabloids have run negative headlines against the British National Party (BNP) on their front page, the most famous in *The Sun*, describing the party as "Bloody Nasty People." This odd love-hate relationship between populist media and politicians, sharing a discourse but not a struggle, is quite common around the world and is a consequence of the fact that even the tabloid media are almost always owned and operated by mainstream forces.

Supranational institutions are also important when it comes to dealing with populist forces. One of the key functions of the EU and the Organization of American States (OAS) is the promotion and protection of (liberal) democracy. In effect, both institutions have on occasions reacted vehemently to the coming to power of populist forces—e.g., the 2000 Austrian coalition government that included the FPÖ—or by some actions undertaken by populist actors—e.g., Fujimori's decision to close the Peruvian parliament in 1992. Nevertheless, the examples of Chávez and Orbán show that supranational institutions have only modest powers vis-à-vis populists. Part of the problem stems from the reluctance of national governments to allow foreign organizations to assess their compliance with liberal democratic standards. Moreover, the criteria for being eligible to join supranational organizations like the EU are of limited help later: once a country becomes a member of the club, it has little capacity to monitor its adherence to democracy and the rule of law. Finally, some populists can actually draw upon international supporters, both populist and nonpopulist, who can shield them from supranational sanctions—as the European People's Party (EPP) does with Orbán—or moderate their impact—as Chávez has done with populist regimes in Ecuador and Nicaragua.

So what can we learn from this short discussion of the main democratic responses to the supply of populist politics? The most relevant lesson is different strategies are available to deal with populism, which mostly fall between the two poles of opposition and cooperation. On the one hand, one has the option to fight back by attacking populist forces and/or ostracizing them. On the other hand, one can try to engage with populists by taking into account (part of) the issues raised by them and/or by including populist forces fully into the political system, for example, by forming a coalition government with them. In the end, no universally best solution exists to respond to populist challengers. All real-life strategies fall somewhere between the two poles of full opposition and full cooperation and in most cases a combination of different strategies is applied.

Which strategy is more effective depends largely on the specific characteristics of both the democracy and the populist challenger. However, two bad approaches, which are unfortunately often suggested, can be identified. First, in many cases establishment actors launch a coordinated frontal attack on the populists. By collectively portraying "them" as "evil" and "foolish," the establishment actors play into the hands of the populists, who can depict their political struggle as "all against one, one against all." Second, some established actors argue that populist actors can be defeated only by adopting part of their populist message—as several western European social democrats have suggested in an attempt to fight off the populist radical right. Both approaches further intensify the moralization and polarization of politics and society, which fundamentally undermines the foundations of liberal democracy.

Populism's illiberal response

Populism is part of democracy. Rather than the mirror image of democracy, however, populism is the (bad) conscience of liberal democracy. In a world that is dominated by democracy and liberalism, populism has essentially become an illiberal democratic response to undemocratic liberalism. Populists ask uncomfortable questions about undemocratic aspects of liberal institutions and policies, such as constitutional courts and international financial institutions, and they give illiberal answers to them, which are often supported by large parts of the population (such as the reintroduction of the death penalty). Liberal democracy has an inherent (potential) tension between the wishes of the majority and the rights of the minority. Traditionally this has led to constitutional courts overruling governments, such as in the famous U.S. Supreme Court cases of *Brown v. Board of Education* (1954) and *Roe v. Wade* (1973), banning segregation and legalizing abortion, respectively. In the past decades unelected bodies and technocratic institutions, such as the European Central Bank (ECB) and the International Monetary Fund (IMF), have established control over important policy domains, thereby seriously limiting the power of elected politicians. Because of the widespread implementation of neoliberal reforms and the adoption of programs such as New Public Management, national governments have become heavily constrained by private companies, transnational organizations, and the (in)visible hand of the market.

Mainstream politicians have willingly implemented these policies but they have rarely tried to sell them to their citizens. Instead, they often present them as necessary, or even inevitable, forced upon the country by powerful foreign organizations (e.g., EU or IMF) and processes (e.g., globalization). As a consequence, little time is spent debating the extent to which at least some of these policies are wrong or can have unintended consequences, which might end up producing more harm than good. In fact, elites have used the growing influence of unelected bodies and technocratic institutions to depoliticize contested political issues, like austerity and immigration, and so minimize the risk of electoral defeat. No better example of this can be cited than the EU, an organization that was consciously constructed to delegate power to institutions that are unelected and therefore largely insulated from popular pressures. It is no wonder, then, that "democratic deficit" has become almost synonymous with the European Union (EU) and that populists are increasingly Euroskeptic. They accuse the national and European elites of having created an all-powerful supranational organization that promotes (neo)liberalism at the expense and against the wishes of the people.

Although populism comes in many different shapes and styles, and mobilizes in very different cultural and political contexts, all populist actors moralize the political debate and try to (re)politicize disregarded issues and groups. While populism often proposes simple solutions to complex problems, anti-populism does so too. Populists constitute complex challenges to all political regimes, including liberal democratic ones. The best way to deal with populism is to engage—as difficult as it is—in an open dialogue with populist actors and supporters. The aim of the dialogue should be to better understand the claims and grievances of the populist elites and masses and to develop liberal democratic responses to them. At the same time, practitioners and scholars should focus more on the message than the messenger. Instead of assuming a priori that populists are wrong, they should seriously examine the extent to which the proposed policies have merit within a liberal democratic regime.

In trying to win over populist supporters, and perhaps even some elites, liberal democrats should avoid both simplistic solutions that pander to "the people" and elitist discourses that dismiss the moral and intellectual competence of ordinary citizens—both will only strengthen the populists. Most importantly, given that populism often asks the right questions but provides the wrong answers, the ultimate goal should be not just the destruction of populist supply, but also the weakening of populist demand. Only the latter will actually strengthen liberal democracy.

References

Chapter 1: What is populism?

Margaret Canovan, *The People* (Cambridge, UK: Polity, 2005).

Rudiger Dornbusch and Sebastian Edwards, eds., *The Macroeconomics of Populism in Latin America* (Chicago: University of Chicago Press, 1992).

Lawrence Goodwyn, *Democratic Promise: The Populist Moment in America* (New York: Oxford University Press, 1976).

Richard Hofstadter, *The Age of Reform: From Bryan to FDR* (New York: Knopf, 1955).

Ghita Ionescu and Ernest Gellner, eds., *Populism: Its Meaning and National Characteristics* (New York: Macmillan, 1969).

Ernesto Laclau, *On Populist Reason* (London: Verso, 2005).

Ernesto Laclau and Chantal Mouffe, *Hegemony and Socialist Strategy: Towards a Radical Democratic Politics* (London: Verso, 1985).

Cas Mudde, "The Populist Zeitgeist." *Government and Opposition* 39.4 (2004): 541–563.

Cas Mudde and Cristóbal Rovira Kaltwasser "Populism," in *The Oxford Handbook of Political Ideologies*, eds. Michael Freeden, Lyman Tower Sargent, and Marc Stears, 493–512 (Oxford: Oxford University Press, 2013).

Carl Schmitt, *Der Begriff des Politischen* (Berlin, Germany: Dunckler & Humblot, 1929).

Paul Taggart, *Populism* (Buckingham, UK: Open University Press, 2000).

Kurt Weyland, "Clarifying a Contested Concept: Populism in the Study of Latin American Politics." *Comparative Politics* 34.1 (2001): 1–22.

Chapter 2: Populism around the world

Carlos de la Torre, *Populist Seduction in Latin America*, rev. ed. (Athens: Ohio University Press, 2010).

Michael Kazin, *The Populist Persuasion: An American History*, rev. ed. (Ithaca, NY: Cornell University Press, 1995).

Kosuke Mizuno and Pasuk Phongpaichit, eds., *Populism in Asia* (Singapore: NUS Press and Kyoto University Press, 2009).

Cas Mudde, *Populist Radical Right Parties in Europe* (Cambridge, UK: Cambridge University Press, 2007).

Cas Mudde and Cristóbal Rovira Kaltwasser, "Exclusionary vs. Inclusionary Populism: Comparing Contemporary Europe and Latin America," *Government and Opposition* 48.2 (2013): 147–174.

Danielle Resnick, *Urban Poverty and Party Populism in African Democracies* (Cambridge, UK: Cambridge University Press, 2013).

Cristóbal Rovira Kaltwasser, "Latin American Populism: Some Conceptual and Normative Lessons," *Constellations* 21.4 (2014): 494–504.

Marian Sawer and Barry Hindess, eds., *Us and Them: Anti-elitism in Australia* (Perth, Australia: API Network, 2004).

Yannis Stavrakakis and Giorgos Katsambekis, "Left-Wing Populism in the European Periphery: The Case of SYRIZA," *Journal of Political Ideologies* 19.2 (2014): 119–142.

Chapter 3: Populism and mobilization

Daniele Albertazzi and Duncan McDonnell, eds., *Twenty-First Century Populism: The Spectre of Western Democracy* (Basingstoke, UK: Palgrave Macmillan, 2008).

Sergio Anria, "Social Movements, Party Organization, and Populism: Insights from the Bolivian MAS," *Latin American Politics & Society* 55.3 (2013): 19–46.

David Art, *Inside the Radical Right: The Development of Anti-immigrant Parties in Western Europe* (Cambridge, UK: Cambridge University Press, 2011).

Paris Aslanidis, "Populist Social Movements of the Great Recession," *Mobilization: An International Quarterly* 21.3 (2016): 301–321.

Julio Carrión, ed., *The Fujimori Legacy: The Rise of Electoral Authoritarianism in Peru* (University Park: Pennsylvania State University Press, 2006).

Catherine Fieschi, *Fascism, Populism, and the French Republic: In the Shadow of the Republic* (Manchester, UK: Manchester University Press, 2004).

Ronald Formisano, *The Tea Party* (Baltimore: Johns Hopkins University Press, 2012).

Kenneth Roberts, "Populism, Political Conflict, and Grass-Roots Organization in Latin America," *Comparative Politics* 36.2 (2006): 127–148.

Elmer E. Schattschneider, *The Semi-sovereign People: A Realist's View of Democracy in America* (New York: Holt, Rinehart and Winston, 1960).

Sidney Tarrow, *Power in Movement: Social Movements and Contentious Politics*, rev. ed. (Cambridge, UK: Cambridge University Press, 2011).

Chapter 4: The populist leader

Kirk A. Hawkins, "Is Chávez Populist? Measuring Populist Discourse in Comparative Perspective," *Comparative Political Studies* 42.8 (2009): 1040–1067.

Karen Kampwirth, ed., *Gender and Populism in Latin America: Passionate Politics* (University Park: Pennsylvania State University Press, 2010).

John Lynch, *Caudillos in Spanish America, 1800–1850* (Oxford: Clarendon, 1992).

Raúl Madrid, "The Rise of Ethnopopulism in Latin America," *World Politics* 60.3 (2008): 475–508.

Cas Mudde and Cristóbal Rovira Kaltwasser, "Populism and Political Leadership," in *The Oxford Handbook of Political Leadership*, edited by R.A.W. Rhodes and Paul 't Hart, 376–388 (Oxford: Oxford University Press, 2014).

Cas Mudde and Cristóbal Rovira Kaltwasser, "Vox Populi or Vox Masculini? Populism and Gender in Northern Europe and South America," *Patterns of Prejudice* 49.1–2 (2015): 16–36.

Paul Taggart, *Populism* (Buckingham, UK: Open University Press, 2000).

Max Weber, *Politik als Beruf* (Stuttgart, Germany: Reclam, 1992 [1919]).

Chapter 5: Populism and democracy

Robert Dahl, *Polyarchy* (New Haven, CT: Yale University Press, 1971).

Ernesto Laclau, *On Populist Reason* (London: Verso, 2005).

Steven Levitsky and Lucan Way. *Competitive Authoritarianism: Hybrid Regimes after the Cold War* (Cambridge, UK: Cambridge University Press, 2010).

Cas Mudde, "The Populist Radical Right: A Pathological Normalcy," *West European Politics* 33.6 (2010): 1167–1186.

Cas Mudde and Cristóbal Rovira Kaltwasser, eds., *Populism in Europe and the Americas: Threat or Corrective for Democracy?* (Cambridge, UK: Cambridge University Press, 2012).

Guillermo O'Donnell and Philippe C. Schmitter, *Transitions from Authoritarian Rule: Tentative Conclusions* (Baltimore: Johns Hopkins University Press, 1986).

Pierre Rosanvallon, *Counter-Democracy: Politics in an Age of Distrust* (Cambridge, UK: Cambridge University Press, 2008).

Cristóbal Rovira Kaltwasser, "The Responses of Populism to Dahl's Democratic Dilemmas," *Political Studies* 62.3 (2014): 470–487.

Kathryn Stoner and Michael McFaul, eds., *Transitions to Democracy: A Comparative Perspective* (Baltimore: Johns Hopkins University Press, 2013).

Charles Tilly, *Democracy* (Cambridge, UK: Cambridge University Press, 2013).

Chapter 6: Causes and responses

Sonia Alonso and Cristóbal Rovira Kaltwasser, "Spain: No Country for the Populist Radical Right?" *South European Society and Politics* 20.1 (2015): 21–45.

Kirk Hawkins, *Venezuela's Chavismo and Populism in Comparative Perspective* (New York: Cambridge University Press, 2010).

Piero Ignazi, "The Silent Counter-Revolution: Hypotheses on the Emergence of Extreme Right-Wing Parties in Europe," *European Journal of Political Research* 22.1 (1992): 3–34.

Inglehart, Ronald. *The Silent Revolution: Changing Values and Political Styles among Western Publics.* Princeton: Princeton University Press, 1977.

Karl Löwenstein, "Militant Democracy and Fundamental Rights, I," *American Political Science Review* 31.3 (1937): 417–432.

Peter Mair, "Representative versus Responsible Government," *MPIfG Working Paper* 8 (2009): 1–19.

Jan-Werner Müller, "Defending Democracy within the EU," *Journal of Democracy* 24.2 (2013): 138–149.

Thomas Payne, *Common Sense* (London: Penguin, 1982 [1776]).

Cristóbal Rovira Kaltwasser and Paul Taggart. "Dealing with Populists in Government: A Framework for Analysis," *Democratization* 23.2 (2016): 201–220.

Wolfgang Streeck, *Buying Time: The Delayed Crisis of Democratic Capitalism* (London: Verso, 2014).

Further reading

Berlet, Chip, and Matthew N. Lyons. *Right-Wing Populism in America: Too Close for Comfort.* New York: Guilford Press, 2000.

Conniff, Michael L., ed. *Populism in Latin America.* 2d ed. Tuscaloosa: University of Alabama Press, 2012.

de la Torre, Carlos, ed. *The Promise and Perils of Populism: Global Perspectives.* Lexington: University of Kentucky Press, 2015.

de la Torre, Carlos, and Cynthia J. Arnson, eds. *Latin American Populism in the Twenty-First Century.* Washington, DC: Woodrow Wilson Center Press, 2013.

Formisano, Ronald. *The Tea Party.* Baltimore: Johns Hopkins University Press, 2012.

Kazin, Michael. *The Populist Persuasion: An American History.* Rev. ed. Ithaca, NY: Cornell University Press, 1998.

Kriesi, Hanspeter, and Takis Pappas, eds. *European Populism in the Shadow of the Great Recession.* Colchester, UK: ECPR Press, 2015.

Laclau, Ernesto. *On Populist Reason.* London: Verso, 2005.

Mudde, Cas. *Populist Radical Right Parties in Europe.* Cambridge, UK: Cambridge University Press, 2007.

Mudde, Cas, and Cristóbal Rovira Kaltwasser, eds. *Populism in Europe and the Americas: Threat or Corrective for Democracy?* Cambridge, UK: Cambridge University Press, 2012.

Panizza, Francisco, ed. *Populism and the Mirror of Democracy.* London: Verso, 2005.

Taggart, Paul. *Populism.* Buckingham, UK: Open University Press, 2000.

Index

Index